D0448805

HITLER'S SECRET WEAPONS
OF MASS DESTRUCTION

HITLER'S SECRET WEAPONS

OF MASS DESTRUCTION

THE NAZI PLAN FOR FINAL VICTORY

MICHAEL FITZGERALD

This edition published in 2019 by Arcturus Publishing Limited
26/27 Bickels Yard, 151–153 Bermondsey Street,
London SE1 3HA

Cover design by Peter Ridley

AD006592UK

Printed in the UK

CONTENTS

INTRODUCTION

Nazi Germany was driven by a desire to dominate the world and create a new master race. Every aspect of life in the Third Reich was focused on the goal of Aryan world domination and science and technology were no exception.

Under the Nazis conventional science and a range of fringe sciences were legitimate areas for research and development. Unorthodox ideas and projects that were too outrageous for other governments to consider received funding. Scientists and others were provided with factories, laboratories, equipment, materials and skilled engineers to test their theories on a practical level. Any tool that might prove useful in achieving world mastery, however unlikely, was examined and tested. There were positive and negative aspects to the Nazi approach to science. It enabled unorthodox ideas to gain a hearing and receive funding but it also led to time, money and resources being wasted on projects that were never capable of realization.

What was it about the Nazi regime that led to this curious and unique attitude towards scientific research and in particular fringe projects? Partly it lay in the schizophrenic attitude towards modernity and technology that pervaded National Socialism. Rejecting liberal humanism and rationalism and distrusting technology and industrialization, the Nazis exalted the ideal of small peasant communities and village life above towns and cities. These were seen as hotbeds of revolt and symptoms of everything they despised and hated about the modern world. The Nazis denounced reason and praised what they called 'thinking with the blood'.

That was the official line but there was also a strongly modernist wing within the Party, led by Goering and Goebbels. This group championed modernism and acclaimed and encouraged science and technology. Himmler and to a lesser extent Hitler had a foot in both camps, paying homage to the

Hitler surrounded by senior members of the Nazi Party in 1933. They were a bizarre bunch. Even the modernizers harked back to an imaginary golden age of Germany, which underpinned their unholy shared faith.

traditionalist message but frequently adopting and encouraging the modernist approach.

During the last six months of the Second World War, it seemed obvious that the Allies had won and the Germans had been crushingly defeated, but in spite of the hopeless military situation Hitler continued to believe that victory could be achieved. He knew his armies were a shadow of their former strength, but he repeatedly told his military advisers and inner circle that Germany possessed *Wunderwaffen* – miracle weapons – that would turn the tide and give the Germans ultimate victory.[1]

News, or at least rumours, of these weapons had also reached the Allies. General George Patton was so concerned about their possible effect that he wrote anxiously in his diary on 4 January 1945, 'We can still lose this war.'[2] In terms of conventional warfare Patton's statement made no sense but German scientists and engineers had made astonishing breakthroughs and possessed at least the theoretical capability of using their scientific discoveries to achieve victory, which made his words more credible.

Was Hitler simply boasting out of desperation or were the 'miracle weapons' real? Had they reached the production stage or were they still only blueprints or even just ideas?

In certain areas, German scientists and engineers led the world. For instance, in aviation research, rocketry and the quest for alternative sources of energy they were supreme. Even in atomic research they were not far behind the British and the Americans.

Acknowledged Nazi secret weapons include the V-1 flying bomb, the V-2 rocket, the V-3 heavy gun and some exceptionally advanced aircraft and anti-aircraft missiles. Some of these devices worked with devastating effect while others failed or, like the V-3 supergun, were destroyed by Allied bombing. Others were not developed in time to be used in combat. A number of the purported miracle weapons were futuristic and more like science fiction than realistic projects. One of the strangest of all these claims is that the Nazis succeeded in creating and piloting a 'flying saucer'.

These claims have largely been dismissed as fantasy but while many of the stories clearly are exercises in creative imagination others are not so easy to dismiss. When the first wave of UFO sightings began in the late 1940s the British aeronautical engineer Sir Roy Fedden commented that the only craft capable of carrying out the manoeuvres attributed to UFOs were some of the Nazi secret weapons. Similar statements were made by other experts in the field.[3]

This does not mean that the Nazis succeeded in developing fully functioning and operational saucer-type craft. Fedden and the others may have been referring to research and projects at the design stage rather than finished products. All the same, the fact that under the constraints of war they were able to devise craft that were 'almost capable', in Fedden's words, of emulating the reported behaviour of early post-war UFOs may be significant.

Following the defeat of Germany many of its leading scientists and engineers were recruited by the Americans and the Russians. Much secret data was undoubtedly stolen by the victorious Allies and a large amount was destroyed during the war. As a result, evidence is fragmentary, often contradictory and always elusive but enough survives to make it plain that some of the many projects on which the Nazis worked appear to have involved disc-type craft.

The extent to which this research was successful will be examined in this book and a study will also be made of the other 'miracle weapons', whether successfully developed or simply at the drawing-board stage. There is no doubt that Nazi scientists contributed decisively to the space programme, but they also began what became post-war projects, which others developed and refined without the constraints of war hindering their research.

FOOTNOTES

1 Henry Stevens, *Hitler's Suppressed and Still-Secret Weapons, Science and Technology*, Adventures Unlimited, 2007
2 Martin Blumenson, *The Patton Papers: 1940–1945*, Da Capo Press, 1996
3 Bill Gunston, *By Jupiter! The Life of Sir Roy Fedden*, Royal Aeronautical Society, 1979

CHAPTER ONE

SCIENTIFIC RESEARCH AND DEVELOPMENT

Self-sufficiency drive

When the Nazis came to power in 1933, the German economy was in recession, with high unemployment and a shortage of raw materials. The currency was weak and, although the regime had promised to bring down unemployment and make the economy strong once more, most observers thought it would be impossible to achieve these aims quickly.

The poverty of the previous four years was one of the main reasons why the German people turned away from the traditional parties and towards the Nazis and the Communists. Cold and hunger were affecting millions of Germans when Hitler came to power and he recognized the need to address these issues urgently. Consequently, the Nazi regime quickly pursued new economic measures and public works programmes to improve the situation and, more importantly for them, their own standing.

Hitler's 'economic miracle' appeared to be working. In 1933, when Hitler became Chancellor, there were six million unemployed and three years later there was full employment. At that point, many Germans regarded 'work and bread' as being a fair exchange for the loss of civil liberties.

In spite of Hitler's lack of knowledge and understanding of science, he grasped the need for scientists and engineers to develop technologically advanced projects to help in his goal of making Germany powerful again. As a result, the Nazis tried many unconventional ideas, some of which proved strikingly successful. Nazi policy was to encourage the development of science and technology as rapidly as possible, primarily with military purposes in mind.

In 1933 Germany had few raw materials and was economically dependent on imports for most of its produce and resources, so the desire for 'autarky' – economic self-sufficiency – was a key policy of the Nazi government. These constraints were at least partly responsible for the willingness of the Nazis to fund the quest for 'alternative' sources of fuel and energy, no matter how bizarre they might appear. The relative shortage of fuel and most other raw materials also encouraged research and development into forms of propulsion that were less reliant upon petrol. As a result, German science began to evolve in an entirely different way from the rest of the world.

The increasing isolation of German scientists and the difficulties of producing raw materials within Germany led to the development of ersatz – substitute – products. Wilhelm Keppler, an industrialist and engineer, was directly appointed by Hitler to identify or create as many alternative or synthetic forms of raw materials such as oils, fats, metals and rubber as possible. Buna (the ersatz rubber) was particularly successful.[1] Synthetic textiles and metals were also developed.

The hope was not only to make Germany self-sufficient in raw materials but also to make the production of military weapons and the manufacturing infrastructure needed to support it as cheap as possible. This objective, combined with the willingness to explore unorthodox scientific ideas, led to numerous experiments that were not even considered worth investigating by the Western powers. Before the war, these experiments were carried out by paid workers and with primarily civilian applications, but once hostilities commenced the focus shifted to largely military purposes and a heavier reliance on slave labour.

Chemists were called upon to create and improve techniques for manufacturing synthetic versions of coffee, petrol and rubber and factories were built to produce these new ersatz products. IG Farben, the chemical and pharmaceutical industry conglomerate, was called upon to lend its expertise, making fundamental contributions to this field.

Synthetic rubber

Germany was the first nation to begin developing synthetic rubber. The team at the Bayer laboratory in Elberfeld, led by award-winning chemist Fritz Hofmann, succeeded in creating isoprene in 1909, the first synthetic rubber.[2] The growing popularity of motor cars led to considerable research being devoted to this field and the First World War acted as a catalyst for its application in other fields. Russia, short of natural rubber resources, invested considerably in developing synthetic alternatives during the war and Germany, faced with a similar problem, also began to develop synthetic rubber for military purposes.

In 1915, German chemists studied the researches of Hofmann and his factory and tried to apply them to armoured vehicles and tanks. They were faced with several difficulties which were never satisfactorily overcome.

The first was that the raw materials necessary for producing methyl isoprene – acetone and aluminium – were more essential in other areas of the war. Acetone was needed to make explosives and aluminium was used to build aircraft motors and airships. The supply of acetone from wood or acetate of lime was limited and synthesizing it from acetic acid was also problematic, because the acetic acid was derived from fermenting grain and grain served as an essential food supply for the troops. After a series of failed trials with rotten potatoes a method involving coal and lime was developed. Three different systems were employed, depending on the intended use of the isoprene. One involved leaving it to stand in tin drums at a temperature of 30 degrees Celsius for between six and 19 weeks. This resulted in the formation of 'H-rubber' – hard rubber. The rubber produced by this process was used in cases for electrical equipment or battery boxes for submarines.

A second method was to place the isoprene in iron drums at 70 degrees Celsius for between three and six months. This led to the production of 'W-rubber' – '*weich*' (soft) – which was used for tyres, hoses, belts and any other products where flexibility was needed. A third method was to allow the isoprene to stand in an atmosphere of carbon dioxide while in contact with sodium wire. This resulted in 'B-rubber', which was used to coat balloon fabric or to insulate wires.

None of these synthetic forms of rubber was adequate but

the Germans had little alternative. They managed to produce 150 tons (136 tonnes) of methyl rubber every month by the end of the war and a total of 2,500 tons (2,268 tonnes) in all. Several factories were built to produce the synthetic material but when the war ended production ceased abruptly. Both the military and the factories knew that the quality of rubber obtained by these processes was inadequate and they returned to the natural product as soon as hostilities were over.[3]

That was the end of the synthetic rubber quest for some years, at least in Germany. Then in 1930 Hermann Staudinger published a paper on developing synthetic rubber. His work was seized upon by the American company Du Pont and on the basis of Staudinger's findings they developed a new material, neoprene.[4]

The Nazis then began to encourage new methods of developing and processing synthetic rubber and by April 1936 the Buna company was set up in Schkopau. The Schkopau factory was part of the Leuna chemical group, yet another subsidiary of the IG Farben industrial complex, and by 1937 it was producing synthetic rubber as well as PVC, THF, acetic acid, acetone, acetic anhydride and trichloroethylene.

During the Second World War the Schkopau plant became the principal producer of synthetic rubber. It also ran the Monowitz-Buna factory section of Auschwitz, where slave workers were forced to produce synthetic oil and rubber. The conditions under which they worked were so extreme that their life expectancy was only a few months.[5]

When the Allies launched the Operation Pointblank series of bombing raids on Germany, the Schkopau factory and other synthetic rubber plants were heavily targeted. Much of the infrastructure was destroyed by the bombing and what remained of the Schkopau plant was captured by the Soviets.[6]

Fuel from coal

The earliest example of the direct conversion of coal into synthetic fuel was developed in Germany by future Nobel Prize winner Friedrich Bergius, who took out a patent for the process in 1913. In 1914 the chemist and entrepreneur Karl Goldschmidt recruited Bergius to build a plant at his factory and by 1919 the production of synthetic fuel from coal had begun.[7] Before long the factories were developing and refining the process and an increasing percentage of German energy needs began to be met by converting coal into synthetic fuel.

The attempt to produce petrol from coal was one key area in which large factories sought to convert one of Germany's few natural resources – coal – into one it lacked – petroleum. Two different techniques were used. One was the Bergius process, which was the method used by IG Farben, and the other was known as the Fischer process. This method of deriving petrol from coal was developed by Dr Franz Fischer of the Kaiser-Wilhelm-Institut für Kohleforschung. Fischer and fellow chemist Hans Tropsch devised their process as early as 1923, turning coal into gas which was then used as a synthetic fuel.

From 1936, the Braunkohle Benzin AG (BRABAG) group of companies also turned out petrol from coal. These processes were carried out at the Leuna works and other factories and the synthetic fuel was sold through the Leuna petrol pumps. By 1937 enough had been manufactured to enable German cars to run on a mixture that was 40 per cent home-produced petrol. The Leuna plant alone produced a third of a million tons a year and by 1938 five new plants had opened to produce petrol from coal.[8] The drive for autarky in fuel and raw materials accelerated as the likelihood of war drew nearer.

During the Second World War the Bergius and Fischer processes were extensively used to produce ersatz oil from coal or water gas. The Bergius plants became the leading source of aviation fuel and other synthetic raw materials or fuels and by 1944 synthetic fuel production resulted in 124,000 barrels of fuel each day from the 25 processing plants. During the war 18 million tons of fuel (16.3m tonnes) were produced from coal or tar sources and a further four million from the Fischer–Tropsch synthesis.[9]

Another way of turning coal into fuel was the Schichau process, in which coal was reduced to a powder. By 1937, it was claimed that this had been successfully achieved. The idea was that by reducing coal to as fine a density as face powder it would be possible for it to behave nearly as effectively as a natural gas. Pieces of coal were crushed between balls or rollers and the raw coal was fed into the pulverizer, together with air heated to an extremely high temperature. The hot air dried the crushed coal and blew the powder out in the form of usable coal fuel, which was then mixed with pre-heated air and expelled via a nozzle to create a kind of 'fuel injection' system. This produced enough heat to ignite the fuel.[10]

In July 1944, because of the extensive destruction of facilities by Allied bombing, the Germans began to develop the 'Cuckoo' project, an underground plant to produce synthetic oil. Construction began north of the Mittelwerk factory (which was built into a hill called the Kohnstein, near Nordhausen) but it was still unfinished when the war ended.[11]

Synthetic fuel was never able to play the dominant role in generating energy that the Nazis hoped. Before the war, they remained hugely dependent on imported oil from Romania and other countries and during the war they ruthlessly stripped the conquered nations of their natural resources to ameliorate the situation in Germany. None of these policies could overcome the fundamental problem of lack of natural resources within Germany, however. In spite of systematic plunder and scientific ingenuity, Germany remained handicapped by the shortage of the raw materials necessary for it to conduct war effectively.

Wood was also processed as a substitute for petrol. The results of these developments were described as 'satisfactory' and in 1937 a German motorist drove from Berlin to London in a car employing 'wood-fuel', at a total cost of ten marks. Nevertheless, more emphasis was placed on processing coal into fuel than using wood and the experiment with wood-fuel made little difference to the problems of creating ersatz petrol.[12]

Bread from air

One of the great ironies of Nazi science is that a German Jew was responsible for some of the most destructive chemicals ever developed and which were used to murder millions in the death camps. In the first instance, though, Fritz Haber was a German chemist who established his reputation by finding a solution to the problem of feeding increasing populations.

Before Haber made his discovery, the supplies of nitrogen necessary to produce greater amounts of food had been imported by ships full of bird excrement or nitrates mined in South America. However, Haber discovered a method of synthesizing ammonia from nitrogen and hydrogen which became an excellent and cheap form of fertilizer. He worked with chemical engineer Carl Bosch to develop what became known as the Haber–Bosch process. At the time this seemed like a miraculous discovery and was referred to as creating 'bread from air'.[13] The new fertilizer was used on an industrial scale and resulted in an extensive increase in crop yields. One observer called it 'the most important technological invention of the twentieth century'.

The Jew who discovered Zyklon-B

With the outbreak of the First World War, Haber, as a patriotic German, became involved in research for the military. The Haber–Bosch process was used to create explosives and Haber also began work on developing a poison gas. He felt that chlorine might be an effective agent of chemical warfare and in 1915 his research resulted in it being used at the Battle of Ypres. Understandably it created widespread horror, but the German authorities were so pleased with its effects that they promoted Haber to the rank of captain in the army. After the war, Haber was given the Nobel Prize for his work on ammonia, but his satisfaction was muted because he was terrified of being arrested as a war criminal for his development of poison gas.

During the 1920s he worked on several projects, including some that were quixotic, such as his plan to extract gold from seawater. After a two-year survey, however, it was concluded that the energy requirement would have far outweighed the gain. More successful, and with a deadly irony, was his research

German scientists dressed for dinner in Göttingen, 1920. In the front row (l to r): Hertha Spon, Ingrid Franck, James Franck, Lise Meitner, Fritz Haber and Otto Hahn. Standing: Albert Einstein, Walter Grotrian, Wilhelm Westphal, Otto von Baeyer, Peter Pringsheim and Gustav Hertz.

into pesticide gases. This work resulted in Zyklon-B, the very chemical agent used by the Nazis to kill Jews and other victims in the gas chambers.

In 1933, with the Nazis in power, Haber was banned from his scientific institute. On arriving for work as usual, the porter denied him access, saying: 'The Jew Haber is not permitted to enter.' The stunned Haber went into exile and died a year later. His legacy remains controversial, with his work on fertilizers being considered by many to be outweighed by his development of poison gas. Haber felt guilty about his part in the use of gas during the First World War and would have been horrified to think that one of his discoveries led to the extermination of millions of people, mainly Jews like himself, in the gas chambers.[14]

German Chemical Society

The DChG – the German Chemical Society – was heavily involved in developing ersatz products and military uses of chemical weapons. Richard Kuhn, one of its leading members, extensively researched tabun and sarin – two toxic nerve gases – and invented a new poison gas known as soman. He was awarded the Nobel Prize in 1938 for his work in chemistry but rejected it.[15]

As well as poison gas the DChG also researched less lethal materials such as polymers. The results of their research were published in a secret journal on chemistry and its military applications, known as the *Reich Berichte* – Reich Reports. During the various Nazi conquests, members of the DChG went into occupied lands and stole equipment, journals and even scientists to help them in their military researches.[16]

Metal carbonyls, for instance, were researched with a view to disabling gas mask filters and Kurt Stantien created a device that was capable of spraying enemy soldiers with poison gas. After the war his research became the basis of a pesticide system for farmers.[17]

Drugged army

The Nazis were interested in any possible 'edge' chemical developments could give them. After the outbreak of the Second World War, it was common practice for German soldiers to be equipped with an amphetamine drug called Pervitin. A factory in Berlin, Temmel, supplied the armed forces with 29 million Pervitin pills between April 1939 and December of the same year. In official documents, it was referred to as 'obm' and its widespread use was a closely guarded secret.

The result of this easy provision of Pervitin was that soldiers became addicted. Doctors at the front raised their concerns about these consequences but their warnings were ignored. As the military situation deteriorated anything that enabled the troops to continue fighting was considered worth persevering with, in spite of the obvious downsides. People, even soldiers, were regarded as expendable by the Nazi leadership and anything that had the potential to prolong the war and stiffen resistance was given the highest priority.

By March 1944 the German army was suffering huge losses, so pharmacologist Gerhard Orchehovsky was put in charge of developing a more effective means of using chemical methods to keep the remaining soldiers fighting longer. He came up with a cocktail of drugs that included Pervitin but added Eukodal (a morphine-based painkiller) and synthetic cocaine produced by the Merk company. The new drug became known as DI-X.

Under a secret project code-named Experiment DI-X, a number of prisoners in Sachsenhausen concentration camp were used as guinea pigs in trials of the drug. Odd Nansen, son of the polar explorer, described seeing 18 inmates of the camp marching on the square where roll-call took place. Under the influence of DI-X, they circled the square continuously, carrying backpacks weighing 20 kilos. They could march up to

90 km (56 miles) a day in this fashion, though most of them died the day after they had been given their drug doses.[18]

Some parts of the German armed forces were supplied with the new 'miracle drug' but not in sufficient quantities to determine how significant its effect was. The war ended before it had been employed on a large enough scale to observe its results. The hope that this new cocktail of chemicals could produce soldiers capable of greater endurance remained unfulfilled.[19]

Harnessing the sun

A bizarre and totally impractical weapon considered by German scientists was the 'sun gun'. The idea of the sun gun was not new. As early as the 16th century, the Scottish mathematician John Napier had suggested using a giant mirror to focus the rays of the sun and set fire to enemy ships.

In 1929 German physicist Hermann Oberth came up with a concept that was worthy of a Bond villain, by proposing a space station with a concave mirror that could reflect sunlight back to the Earth.[20] It was clear that his invention was not intended to benefit mankind by providing unlimited sunshine:

> My space mirror is like the hand mirrors that schoolboys use to flash circles of sunlight on the ceiling of their classroom. A sudden beam flashed on the teacher's face may bring unpleasant reactions.

During the war this idea was taken up by the Nazis, who recognized its military potential. Scientists at the German army artillery proving grounds at Hillersleben then set about creating a 'supergun' using the sun's energy. Building on Oberth's original notion, their idea was that it would form part of a space station that would orbit over 5,000 miles (8,000 km) above Earth. They believed a reflector made of sodium and with an area of 3.5 sq miles (9 sq km) would be able to generate enough focused heat to destroy a city or even make an ocean boil. The only problem was that the world's first space station would not be launched until 1971 – by the Russians – so they were a little ahead of their time.

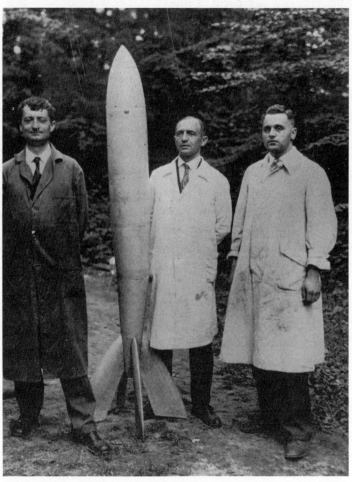

German inventor Hermann Oberth (left) with two colleagues at the Jungerheide research station in 1931. It was claimed that their rocket, later recognized as the forerunner of the V-2, would be capable of carrying mail from Berlin to New York in 24 minutes.

After the war, in response to queries from Allied investigators, the scientists concluded that it would have taken between fifty and a hundred years to complete the 'sun gun' – many years after Hitler's short-lived Reich had met its inglorious end.[21]

The V-3 'super cannon'

The sun gun brings us neatly to the V-3 'super cannon', which was a more feasible Nazi wonder weapon. In an attempt to hide its real purpose, the V-3 heavy gun was known as the *Hochdruckpumpe* (high pressure pump), but it was in fact a multi-barrelled cannon – the largest artillery weapon ever built.

This was the only Nazi 'wonder weapon' that was not originated by German scientists. During the First World War Krupps developed the 'Paris gun', which was capable of bombarding Paris from the German positions at a distance of 78 miles (126 km). It was nicknamed 'Big Bertha' by the Allies. The French were alarmed by this weapon and developed their own multi-chambered heavy gun to respond, but when the Germans retreated and then surrendered, the French gun never advanced beyond the blueprint stage.[22]

Following the collapse of France in 1940, the plans for the weapon were discovered and the German engineer August Cönders became interested in the shelved French project. He had already devised the Röchling artillery shell and believed that the French design could provide him with a long-range gun. Cönders knew that projecting shells at high speed from conventional guns led to a rapid deterioration of the tubes, so his idea was to place many small charges along the length of the gun barrel to achieve long-range penetration without contributing to the accelerated obsolescence of the gun tube.[23]

He suggested using electrical charges to activate the weapon and then built a 20 mm (0.8 in) prototype multi-chamber gun and began test firing it. The results were encouraging but

Cönders needed the approval of the German military before he could develop the concept further, so in early 1943 the factory owner Hermann Röchling went to Albert Speer and explained how Cönders had come up with the idea of a 'supercannon' that could direct massive and concentrated firepower against London from Calais.[24] Speer needed little persuasion. England would be shelled into submission in a matter of days and it could all be achieved without leaving France. After talking to Hitler, he quickly gave his approval for the construction and testing of a prototype and Cönders began work near Magdeburg. However, he soon encountered serious problems with the design and operation of the weapon. The muzzle velocity was much slower than he had imagined and it frequently failed to fire.

These technical difficulties did not deter Speer from authorizing the building of a V-3 cannon on the island of Wolin in the Baltic, as well as beginning construction on the main launch site in France in September 1943. In March 1944, the project was brought under direct German army control but the technical problems continued. Six companies were commissioned to produce projectiles for the cannon and May 1944 saw trials at Wolin, which continued until July. Results were mixed, however, and on 4 July the gun burst during its latest testing.

Construction of the main launch site took place at Mimoyecques near Cap Gris Nez, about 8 miles (12.9 km) away from Calais. Work began with the building of railway lines to supply the site and by October 1943 the task of excavating shafts to house the guns began.

It was planned that the site would contain 50 guns in total, which would be housed, together with the ammunition, in underground galleries dug out of the hill and served by an underground railway. There was an extensive network of tunnels and armoured doors to protect the complex.[25] The intention was to have the guns fully operational by October 1944 but further failed tests slowed the operation's progress.

An agent reported the existence of the launch site to British intelligence almost immediately and described it as a 'rocket launching cannon', but this information was dismissed as scaremongering. In the absence of any more precise information, the Allies assumed that the site was going to be used for launching V-2 rockets. It was not until late 1944 that the British authorities finally realized that the agent's information had been correct. Even then they had no idea where the weapon was located.[26] It was only after the war that the full extent of the threat became known. In a trembling voice Winston Churchill declared that the site could have been responsible for the 'most devastating attack of all on London'.

However, while no one knew for sure what the Germans were doing it was clear that something big was happening, so several bombing raids took place between November 1943 and June 1944. The raids did not have much effect, though Joe Kennedy Junior, JFK's brother, died on one of the missions. It was at this point that an invention by Barnes Wallis, one of Churchill's scientists, was brought into the equation. The Tallboy bomb had been designed for deep penetration of an underground target, so it was ideally suited to the task. Housed in armour-piercing casing, it contained 3 tons (2.72 tonnes) of high explosive and was capable of penetrating 5 m (16.4 ft) of reinforced concrete.

On 6 July 1944, 19 Lancaster bombers from 617 Squadron – better known as 'the Dam Busters' – dropped 35 tons (31.75 tonnes) of the high-explosive Tallboy bombs. The Allies did not know if these experimental bombs had destroyed the target, but they had damaged it sufficiently to make the site unusable. On 8 July an engineer working on the project reported that the raid had destroyed all chance of the complex being used as a launching base for the gun.[27]

Speer and Hitler refused to accept the engineer's assessment that the project was no longer viable and instead ordered the guns to be moved into Germany. They were transferred from the control of the army to the SS. The V-3 finally entered active service in a much-reduced capacity during the 'Battle of the Bulge' in December 1944. Seven rounds of shells were fired from the first gun tube on 30 December and 183 further rounds were fired from the second tube between 11 January 1945 and 22 February 1945, with the gun aimed at Luxembourg. Only 142 rounds hit the target and the total casualties caused by the weapon were ten fatalities and 35 injuries.[28]

If the V-3 had not been destroyed by the Tallboy bombs it is possible that the Germans might have been able to overcome the technical difficulties. The weapon had two main defects. One was its lack of range – it was impossible for it to have hit London, which was the primary target of the gun – and the other was the difficulty of successfully firing shells with sufficient explosive power. There was widespread scepticism about the project from senior military officers from the outset, but Hitler and Speer dismissed their objections.

Perhaps the V-3 was a throwback to the days of a more static role for artillery. The Second World War showed that mobile artillery units were more effective than heavy but slow weapons like the V-3 'super cannon'.

Weight problem

Just as with the V-3, the Nazis were convinced that the army with the heaviest weapons would win the day. In their eyes it stood to reason that if a very large gun could be moved around the battlefield at the speed of a tank the enemy would soon be destroyed. Following this plan, a team of German engineers designed the the *Jägdtiger* (hunting tiger), a tank destroyer that was the heaviest armoured fighting vehicle used during the war. It remains the weightiest armoured vehicle ever to enter production.

The Germans had made earlier attempts at producing tank destroyers, such as the *Marder I, II* and *III* and the *Sturmgeschütz* (StuG) *III* (the StuG III was built on the chassis of a Panzer III tank and was the most-produced armoured vehicle in the Second World War). All were successful in their role, so the German army became interested in the idea of self-propelled guns.

In early 1942, the Wehrmacht began to investigate the idea of mounting a suitable 128 mm (5 in) gun on a self-propelled tank chassis. It was intended to be used as a tank destroyer rather than in a support role for infantry and test firing of the gun demonstrated its accuracy and power.

By October 1943 the gun was installed on a *Tiger II* tank and displayed to Hitler. One version had an eight-wheel Porsche suspension system while another used Henschel torsion bar suspension with nine road wheels on each side. This prototype was completed in February 1944.

The final version, the *Jägdtiger*, was based on a modified version of the *Tiger II* tank to which a box-like superstructure had been added. It was extremely heavily armour-plated, with almost ten inches of armour at the front of the vehicle, and was armed with a 128 mm Pak 44 L/55 gun that had greater range and power than any Allied tank. But with cost, weight and shortage of raw materials all factors in its construction, the *Jägdtiger* was fitted with a fixed casement rather than movable turrets. As a result, the gun was limited in range, with only ten degrees of turn, and only by moving the entire tank could it be fired outside that traverse. The projectile and the explosive charge for the gun had to be loaded separately.

There were many technical problems with the *Jägdtiger*. The heavy vehicle (weighing around 71 tonnes [78 tons]) was slow-

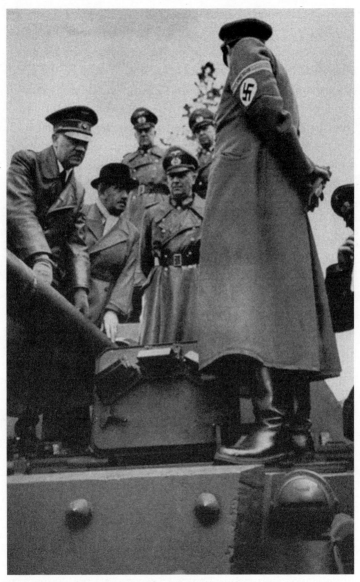

Heavy metal: Adolf Hitler, Ferdinand Porsche, Walter Buhle and Albert Speer inspect a Jägdtiger *hot off the production line from the factory at Rügenwalde in Pomerania (now Darlowo, Poland), March 1943.*

moving and prone to break down when it was moved and the gun had to be permanently locked in place to avoid wearing out the brackets, which would have prevented accurate firing. A tactical problem for its crews was that in spite of the tank's immense weight the weak point of the design was its armour. From the front it was almost invulnerable, but the side armour was thinner and could be penetrated by enemy tank guns.[29]

One hundred and fifty *Jägdtiger*s were ordered and 88 of them were produced between July 1944 and March 1945. Eleven were manufactured with Porsche suspension and the remainder used the Henschel system.[30]

Two heavy anti-tank battalions were equipped with *Jägdtiger*s from September 1944 onwards, but Allied domination in the air made it difficult for the heavy and cumbersome vehicles to move. The *Jägdtiger* commander Otto Carius stated that the technical problems with the device and the inexperience of the crews meant that the full potential of the weapon was never realized.[31] Twenty per cent of them were destroyed during the fighting.

The *Jägdtiger*s were last used in action on 15 April 1945 and were relatively successful, destroying around 20 Allied tanks and over 30 other vehicles. The *Jägdtiger* may have been slow and ponderous but if the crews ensured that the front of the vehicle faced the enemy it was unstoppable.

Mice

However, the *Jägdtiger* was a mere lightweight compared with the super heavy tanks that were designed during the war. The origin of the super tanks lay in a 1941 strategic study carried out by Krupp, which involved examining the designs of Russian heavy tanks. As a result of this survey one of Krupp's directors suggested a thousand-ton tank. The idea was forwarded to Hitler who approved it almost immediately. He was obsessed with big, heavy weapons, the bigger the better, even if they drained ill-afforded resources to little effect.

The first result of this research was the Panzer VIII *Maus* (Mouse) super heavy tank.

The *Maus* was 33 ft 6 in long (10.2 m), 12 ft 2 in wide (3.71 m) and 11 ft 9 in high (3.58 m). It weighed 188 tons (170 tonnes) and like the *Jägdtiger* it carried a 128 mm gun (5 in), a powerful weapon that could destroy any Allied vehicles that strayed into its path.

The *Maus* was planned to enter production in the middle of 1943, when ten vehicles a month would be produced, but on 1 May Hitler viewed a wooden model of the *Maus* and demanded an increase in its weight and armament.[32]

By December 1943 the first prototype *Maus* was produced without a turret. Six months of testing followed before a production turret and armament were added.[33] However, the weight of the *Maus* made it unsuitable for crossing bridges so it was then redesigned as an amphibious vehicle. The idea was that it would ford rivers and if necessary submerge before reappearing on land. A snorkel was fitted to the vehicle to allow this mode of operation.

Further tests took place on the modified vehicle in September 1944, but only two of the super tanks were successfully built and they never saw combat. One was partially destroyed by German troops as the Soviet forces advanced and the Russians captured the other vehicle and transported it to the Soviet Union. It is now on display in the Kubinka Tank Museum, Moscow.

Rats

If the *Maus* was too heavy at 188 tons then the super heavy tanks that followed it were concepts that defied logic. The idea for the *Landkreuzer P-1000 Ratte* (Landcruiser Rat) was proposed in June 1942 by Krupp and was followed by detailed blueprints in December 1942.

The *Ratte* was another project about which Hitler was enthusiastic while others were dubious. It was proposed to arm it with naval strength artillery – a 280 mm 5h C/28 gun, just like the one that was used on the battleship *Gneisenau* – and to protect it with 10 in (24.4 cm) of heavy steel, so that it would be invulnerable to conventional weapons. The problem was that like the dinosaurs it was just too big to survive. At 115 ft long, 36 ft high and 46 ft wide (35 x 11 x 14 m), it would have weighed 1,000 tons (907 tonnes), making it five times heavier than the *Maus*. Its gun alone would have weighed 100 tons (90.7 tonnes).

Most Nazi leaders supported the project for the *Maus*, but it was a different story when it came to the *Ratte*. The sheer size and weight of the vehicle would have made it impossible for it to cross bridges or most roads as its mass would have wrecked them. It would also have been a highly visible target from the air, it was too heavy to be transported by road or rail and it was too wide to use tunnels. Guderian dismissed the project with the words: 'Hitler's fantasies sometimes shift into the gigantic.'[34]

During the design stage of the project the idea for a 'super gun' was put forward. The *Landkreuzer P.1500 Monster* would have been a self-propelled siege gun that weighed a third more, at 1,500 tons (1,360 tonnes), than even the impossibly heavy *Ratte*. It was proposed that the *Monster* would be armed with an 800 mm (31.5 in) Dora/Schwerer Gustav K (E) gun, which would have the ability to discharge shells without directly engaging with the enemy.

The *Maus* and the *Ratte* had already shown the problems of such large and heavy vehicles. They could not be transported by road or rail, they destroyed roads and bridges with their weight and their mass meant that they were slow-moving and therefore vulnerable to attack.

A combination of these factors led Speer to cancel all three projects in 1943. For all their firepower and heavy armour they would have been impractical if used in combat. Not even a prototype of the *Ratte* or the *Monster* was built.[35]

Weapons procurement in the Third Reich

The HWA (*Heereswaffenamt* – Army Weapons Agency) was primarily in charge of procuring army equipment, weapons and ammunition. It also had responsibility for military research and development. The *Abnahme* (Army Acceptance Organization) was the division of the HWA specifically charged with the re-armament of Germany. By 1940, the *Abnahme* had five departments and employed 25,000 men. They tested all equipment, weapons and ammunition before those items were delivered to the army.

General Karl Becker was an adviser to the HWA. He was an early supporter of rockets and in 1929 was authorized by the Reich Ministry of Defence to develop rockets as weapons. Dornberger and von Braun worked for him before moving on to specifically rocket-based projects.

In November 1933, Becker became head of the weapons testing office and the research department. On 4 February 1938, he was appointed head of the HWA. Becker was a scientist in his own right and held professorships in military science, technical physics, defence technology and ballistics. He was the first army officer to be admitted to the PAW (Prussian Academy of Sciences).

In 1940, Hitler criticized him for not manufacturing weapons at the rapid pace he demanded. The depressed

Becker committed suicide after these rebukes, but his death was covered up and he was given a state funeral.

From 1933 to 1939, Fritz Todt built the vast autobahn network. With the coming of war in 1939, Todt's responsibilities changed and in 1940 he became Minister of Armaments and Munitions. His first major wartime project was the Westwall, known to the British as the Siegfried Line. In 1941, he constructed the Atlantic Wall and fortified the Channel Islands.

In spite of his strong support for the Nazis, Todt was an independent thinker and in February 1942 bluntly told Hitler that he would lose the war with the Soviet Union. Soon after, Todt died in a plane crash and there has been speculation that he was murdered for his presumption, but this seems unlikely.

On his death, Speer took over Organization Todt and in 1943 merged it with his Ministry of Armaments and War Production. Speer used it to construct platforms for launching V-1s and V-2s as well as building air raid shelters and underground complexes.

Hitler's direct involvement in military procurement was limited. Ernst Udet was responsible for most of the Luftwaffe's procurement and the HWA for the majority of the armed services' needs. Goering and Hitler took an interest in particular projects but on the whole their involvement tended to make matters worse. Both men failed to appreciate the qualities of the revolutionary German fighters being developed and insisted that they should be used primarily as bombers.

Hitler as an infantryman might have had some excuse for his failure to see their virtues. It is less easy to excuse Goering, a former fighter pilot in the First World War and who took over from Baron Manfred von Richthofen

– the 'Red Baron' – when he was finally killed. He had promised Hitler that he would destroy the British forces at Dunkirk through air power alone and failed miserably. The Battle of Britain was another disastrous failure on his part.

Speer was a different matter and his intelligence and eye for detail meant that projects in which he was involved were generally completed successfully. He trusted his technical and scientific teams and generally let them develop the weapons without too much unnecessary interference.

The mutual jealousy between Nazi leaders and departments hampered the war effort. Another problem was Hitler's stubbornness. When in 1941 Speer tried to persuade him to concentrate more on the war effort and in particular to mobilize the civilian population as a whole, his efforts were rebuffed. Speer remarked:

While concerned minions look on, Adolf Hitler, Fritz Todt (centre) and Albert Speer (far right) loom over the architectural model for a section of autobahn at the Schaffendes Volk *('constructive people') Exhibition in Düsseldorf, 1937.*

It was quite extraordinary how adamantly he opposed this. By this time we knew that – quite contrary to us – Britain had fully mobilized, including putting women into factories and uniforms. It was totally impossible, and remained impossible to the end, to persuade Hitler that in total war women had to work in war production.

By November 1941, a combination of the Russian winter and dogged Soviet resistance had led the underprepared and underequipped German army to a crisis point. Tanks and weapons froze and, with the virtual breakdown of transport facilities in occupied Russia, it became nearly impossible to supply the troops. Bridges, roads, railways and factories were deliberately destroyed by the retreating Soviet army.

Speer begged Hitler to let him send his construction teams and those of Organization Todt to repair the railways in Russia. It took Todt and Speer weeks of frantic appeals before he relented and allowed them to send their workers in to rebuild the damage.

Speer's takeover of Organization Todt following Todt's death created a conflict between him and Goering. Goering had resented Todt's power and wanted to add it to his own empire now that his rival was dead. Hitler's choice of Speer to take over Todt's functions infuriated Goering.

Speer's appointment transformed the situation for the better. Goering's inefficiency meant that Hitler not only passed on Todt's duties to Speer but also put him effectively in charge of military procurement. He knew that radical changes in the system of weapons procurement were necessary and Speer, having secured the support of Hitler and Bormann, began to reorganize the structure.

Goering had allowed army bureaucrats to dominate the procurement process. Speer assigned responsibility for individual projects to firms and factories directly. Guns, tanks, aircraft, submarines, missiles and other weapons programmes were produced in single sites. Speer put technicians and engineers in charge rather than business or army leaders. As Speer said, 'The development of new tanks was put in the hands of Ferdinand Porsche, and that of guns in those of Professor Karl Müller.'

He also began gearing industry towards the needs of war. Speer drafted a 'Decree for the Protection of the Armaments Industry' which was signed by Hitler. It declared that:

> In the deployment of existing manpower, absolute priority is to be given to the requirements of war. The same applies for the distribution of raw materials and products essential to the war economy.

May 1942 saw another radical change in German weapons production and procurement. That month Speer was taken by General Friedrich Fromm to meet with a small group of German scientists. Among them were Hahn and Heisenberg. Heisenberg told them that his team had been working since 1938 on the development of an atomic bomb. They were hampered in their task by the loss of Jewish scientists and the drafting of gifted young scientists into the armed forces. Their project was also underfunded.

Speer, impressed by the possibilities of the weapon, asked what they needed to continue their research more effectively. He was told that they would like scientists to be exempted from military service, better facilities, steel and nickel (both restricted metals) and a few hundred thousand marks to build a cyclotron.

Speer offered the team far more than they requested, but Heisenberg told him that they needed to conduct further small experiments before they were ready for 'the big one'.

Speer knew that Hitler despised science and in particular 'Jewish physics'. He decided not to tell Hitler or the other leading Nazis about the atomic project and managed to keep it a secret for some considerable time. He was less successful in concealing the rocket programme, though he managed to keep Hitler ignorant of it for some months.

From 1942, Speer was the primary channel for approval of military procurement and until 1944, when he began to lose favour with Hitler, his policies were generally followed. After that, he struggled against an increasingly irrational insistence by Hitler that heavy bombers, rockets and the atomic bomb could bring the Germans victory. The time when Speer was in undisputed control of military procurement and scientific development saw the German war effort at its most successful and productive.

The rocket research and development programmes were largely ignored by Hitler until 1942. At that point, he suddenly decided that they could change the course of the war and issued a series of unrealistic demands for rapid development and use of projects that were still in the experimental stage. Even so, while his interference caused problems it was intermittent. In spite of Hitler's complete lack of understanding of science and modern technology, the scientists and engineers working on their cutting-edge projects were still able to achieve remarkable results.

FOOTNOTES

1 Stephen H. Roberts, *The House That Hitler Built*, Methuen, 1937

2 http://matrikel.uni-rostock.de/id/200026068/

3 Mark Michalovic, *Destination Germany: A Poor Substitute*, http://www.pslc.ws/macrog/exp/rubber/synth/methyl.htm/

4 John K. Smith, 'The Ten-Year Invention: Neoprene and Du Pont Research 1930–1939', *Technology and Culture*, 26 (1): 345–355

5 Frank A. Howard, *Buna Rubber: The Birth of an Industry*, D. van Nostrand Company, 1947

6 Major Gene Gurney, *The War in the Air: A Pictorial History of World War II Air Forces in Combat*, Bonanza Books, 1962

7 Anthony N. Stranges, 'Friedrich Bergius and the Rise of the German Synthetic Fuel Industry', *Isis, The History of Science Society*, 75 (4): 643–667

8 H. Schulz, 'Short history and present trends of Fischer–Tropsch synthesis', *Advance Catalysis*, 1999, 186 (1–2): 3–12

9 Anthony N. Stranges, 'Germany's Synthetic Fuel Industry 1927–1945', *Energia*, 12 (5): 2001

10 'Pulverised Coal to Run Ships Rival Oil as Fuel', *Popular Mechanics*, May 1929

11 'Minutes of Meeting No 45/6', Enemy Oil Intelligence Committee, 6 February 1945

12 Roberts, op. cit.

13 T. Hager, *The Alchemy of Air*, Harmony Books, 2008

14 Chris Bowlby, 'The Chemist of Life and Death', BBC Radio 4, 12 April 2011

15 Brian Lukey and Harry Salem, *Chemical Warfare Agents: Chemistry, Pharmacology, Toxicology, and Therapeutics*, CRC Press, 2007

16 Sarah Everts, 'Chemistry in Nazi Germany', *Chemical and Engineering News*, 91 (37): 30–33

17 Ibid.

18 Jeevan Vasagar, 'Nazis tested cocaine on camp inmates', *Guardian*, 19 November 2002

19 Semyon Tsur, 'Nazis Tried to Chemically Enhance Their Soldiers', *Kirier-WebPravda.ru*, 2-16-3

20 'Science: Sun Gun', *Time Magazine*, 9 July 1945

21 'The German Space Mirror', *Life Magazine*, 23 July 1945

22 Paul Wood and Roger Ford, *Germany's Secret Weapons in World War II*, Zenith, 2000

23 Peter Thompson, *The V-3 Pump Gun*, ISO Publications, 1999

24 David Irving, *The Mare's Nest*, William Kimber, 1964

25 Steven J. Zaloga, Hugh Johnson and Chris Taylor, *German V-Weapon Sites 1943–45*, Osprey, 2008

26 Christy Campbell, *Target London: Under Attack from the V-Weapons*, Little, Brown, 2012

27 Ibid.

----

28 Stephen Bull, 'V3', *Encyclopedia of Military Technology and Innovation*, Greenwood Press, 2004

29 Peter Chamberlain and Hilary L. Doyle, *Encyclopedia of German Tanks of World War Two*, Arms and Armour, 1999

30 Chris Bishop, *The Encyclopedia of Weapons of World War II*, MetroBooks, 2002

31 Otto Carius, *Tigers in the Mud*, Stackpole Books, 2003

32 Heinz Guderian, *Panzer Leader*, Penguin, 2009 (first published 1950)

33 Thomas Jentz, *Panzer Tracts No. 6-3 Schwere Panzerkampfwagen Maus and E-20 Development and Production from 1942 to 1945*, Darlington Publications, 2008

34 Chamberlain and Doyle, op. cit.

35 David Porter, *Hitler's Secret Weapons, 1933–1945: The Essential Facts and Figures for Germany's Secret Weapon Programme*, Amber Books, 2010

CHAPTER TWO

AVIATION DEVELOPMENT

The Luftwaffe spreads its wings

Under the terms of the Treaty of Versailles Germany was forbidden to possess an air force, so it had been difficult for German military aviation to develop as rapidly as in other countries. Consequently, when the Nazis came to power in Germany they put scientific, military and aviation research at the forefront of their programme of re-armament.

The 1930s was a time when the major countries were developing new types of aircraft. Two of those nations, Britain and Italy, were the world leaders in aeronautical development. During the 1920s Britain and Italy had been the main countries contesting the Schneider Trophy, which was designed to push the boundaries of aircraft performance for flying boats and seaplanes. Britain won the final contest in 1931 with its Supermarine S6 seaplane, but the Italians were not able to enter that year. Had they done so, their own Macchi-Castoldi aeroplane would almost certainly have won. It was the most advanced seaplane in the world and went on to break many speed records.[1]

German aviation languished during the 1920s. Civil aircraft were built and flying clubs were popular but the ban on an air force meant that any kind of military aviation development was impossible. Illegal flights of military planes took place in collaboration with Soviet Russia but the Luftwaffe as such was no more than a hope for the future.

With Hitler's appointment as German Chancellor in January 1933, the situation changed dramatically. From the moment he came to power, Hitler gave German military aviation top priority and the Air Ministry was ordered to make plans to build 1,000 war planes.

Pilots were rapidly trained and aeronautical factories such as Messerschmitt and Heinkel were ordered to construct new, advanced planes for the resurgent Luftwaffe. With the growing emphasis on re-armament under the Nazis, the military side of aviation was given huge public funding. Work on every possible project that might increase the speed and warlike capabilities of aircraft and missiles was encouraged. German fighter and bomber planes developed rapidly under the Third Reich and less orthodox scientific projects considered to have a possible military application also received funding. Among them were ideas either at the fringes of orthodox science or those based on entirely pseudo-scientific concepts.

The Luftwaffe was first tested during the Spanish Civil War, when it provided invaluable air support to Franco's rebels and notoriously destroyed Guernica by means of aerial bombardment. Foreign observers were impressed by the quality of the new German air force and governments across the world became concerned at its rapidly improving capability.

Hermann Goering took over as head of the Luftwaffe in 1935. Failing to show the detailed attention he always paid to his tailoring, he lacked technical know-how and sensible forward planning. In 1940, he shifted focus from bombing British airfields to terrorizing towns and cities; this allowed the RAF to reorganize and ultimately to win the Battle of Britain.

The bulk of aviation research and production was concentrated on fighters and bombers for the Luftwaffe. Most of these planes were constructed on entirely conventional principles though attempts were constantly made to improve their performance and refine their design.

Ghost fliers

In 1935 Britain announced that it was going to strengthen the RAF, which prompted Hitler to respond by revealing the existence of the Luftwaffe. As Hitler had expected, the reaction of the rest of the world was lukewarm. Nevertheless, he felt that it would be safer not to alarm Britain and the other powers at this early stage, so the size and composition of the new Luftwaffe was kept secret. Hermann Goering, a former fighter pilot during the First World War with 22 official victories to his name, was placed in charge of Germany's new air force.

It was perhaps no coincidence that between 1933 and 1936 'ghost aircraft' were seen, principally over Scandinavia. The years 1933 and 1934 saw a large 'wave' of 'ghost fliers' being observed and reported and there was then a brief lull before another surge of sightings took place in 1936.[2] These aircraft tended to fly over railways, towns, ships and military installations. Some witnesses described them as enormous four-engined machines, though on one occasion a plane with eight propellers was reported.

Scandinavia had almost no private planes and both military and civil aircraft were still very much in the development stage in that part of the world. However, a three-engined Fokker had flown to the North Pole in 1926 and this flight was often compared by Scandinavian witnesses to the aircraft they saw in the sky. The first reported case of ghost fliers took place in November 1933, when the inhabitants of Västorbotten in Sweden described seeing unusually bright lights at night. They were observed in the distance and appeared to follow the valley in the direction of Norway. When these lights continued to appear, investigations were made and it was discovered that they must be coming from aircraft. This was a mystery to the Swedish authorities, as the only aircraft ever seen in that remote vicinity were an 'ambulance plane' for emergency and rescue work or customs and border patrol aeroplanes. At the time of the sightings no border or customs aeroplanes were in the area and the ambulance plane was being repaired. What is more, the army and the air force had no planes or bases in the vicinity.

The possibility of an aircraft being engaged in smuggling was the first theory to be considered. To investigate this idea customs planes began searching the area, but in spite of all these aerial patrols nothing was found. The volume of reports of strange lights increased and soon the sound of aircraft engines and searchlight beams were also notified to the authorities. The area of these observations also expanded to as far afield as the Baltic coast. As many as five sightings of lights a day were made but it was not until New Year's Eve 1933 that an aircraft was first observed.[3]

On that day Olav Hedlund was sitting at home in Sorsele, Swedish Lapland, when he heard a plane above his head. There was a bright moon that night, so when he looked outside he was able to see a grey-coloured aircraft without markings or identification and flying at around 1,300 ft (396 m). It circled the railway station before heading north, following the line of the railway tracks.

Almost a year later, in December 1933, a report of a strange aircraft was received from Sweden. Its lights had covered the entire area before it disappeared to the west. Then in January 1934 a curate in northern Sweden reported that he had seen the ghost fliers for over two years. The previous year 12 had flown over his village, always travelling from south-west to north-east. On four occasions, the grey-coloured machines had flown close to the ground but no markings could be distinguished, though he could see they were monoplanes. One of the planes had passed directly over his rectory and he had observed three people sitting in the cockpit. There were so many reports of these aircraft being sighted that the Swedish air force became involved. When the 'ghost fliers', as they swiftly became known, were spotted over an isolated part of Sweden the air force launched 24 planes to search for them, assisted by search parties on land and at sea. Two planes crashed during the operation, which was conducted under extremely severe weather conditions.

In spite of the difficulties they had encountered during their last operation, in February 1934 the Swedish air force once more had to take to the skies in search of a mystery aircraft. A number of people had reported seeing a shining light at an altitude of 1,200 ft (366 m). Whatever it was then turned and flew away. Observers had also reported hearing noises in the sky above them. Sometime later the same phenomenon was observed in Norway. Witnesses there seem to have been convinced that the noise came from a plane of some sort because they all agreed that the engines had been shut down three times while it was directly overhead. It had flown low enough to deluge the whole region with brilliant light.

There were also reports from Norway that two 'ghost fliers' had landed. The first Norwegian landing took place on an island and the second in the far north. Both were in isolated areas of the country. Observers heard loud engines and saw blinding lights, which looked like searchlights, according to witnesses. One machine landed in the water and stayed there for around an hour or so, during which time its lights had gone out. The Norwegian navy sent a ship to investigate but by the time of its arrival the aircraft had vanished.

Ghost fliers were never seen taking off nor could any bases for them be identified, yet they had been observed over an area covering more than a third of Sweden's territory. If they were indeed German aircraft, how did they carry enough fuel for such long flights? As reports of boats and ships being seen in the waters began to be received, speculation grew about the possibility of the planes being launched from an aircraft carrier somewhere off the coast. Once more the Swedish air force tried to investigate, but no trace of the intruders was ever found. One of the more interesting of these accounts comes from Norway on 28 January 1934. Captain Sigvard Olsen testified in an official report, supported by the testimony of another sailor who was also called Olsen, that while they were on board the freighter *Tordenskjoldand,* a seaplane suddenly appeared in front of the ship's bow. It was night-time and the ship was sailing between two Arctic ports. Olsen told the inquiry:

> When he reached only a few metres from the ship, the plane turned to the right and flew directly over it. A beam of light swooped over the deck, turning darkness into broad daylight for 15–20 seconds. The plane was a great greyish machine exactly like the French plane of the Latham type which Roald Amundsen used on his last expedition. In the cabin of the craft Captain Olsen saw a person, probably the pilot, dressed in some sort of 'anorak'. He wore big glasses and had a hood over his head. The machine had no marks or insignia. It circled once around the vessel and then vanished.

A sighting over Helsinki in Finland baffled the Finnish authorities. The report stated:

> Continued night flights over North Finland, Sweden and Norway, by so-called 'ghost aviators', which

have caused so much apprehension already as to prompt the General Staff to organize reconnoitring on a wide scale by Army planes, all over Northern Finland, still remain a deep mystery. According to one expert's theory, the first of the ghost aviators was a Japanese, scouting the Arctic region, whose activities caused the Soviets to despatch aeroplanes to watch the Japanese. The Soviet authorities, however, deny this theory.

The governments of Norway, Sweden and Finland became alarmed by these mysterious phenomena. There were so many reports of the ghost fliers that there could be no question of isolated craft. It seemed that a large-scale violation of Scandinavian airspace was taking place, so the three countries decided to launch a joint investigation of the events.

Witnesses' descriptions of the planes, though not entirely consistent, appeared to point to the fact that they were larger and more advanced than the most sophisticated military aircraft known. Not only that, but their ability to operate under extreme weather conditions and across even the most dangerous mountain areas meant that there must have been bases somewhere where they could be refitted, refuelled and maintained. No bases of any kind were ever found, however, and the baffled Swedish military were forced to issue a public statement. They said that their airspace had been repeatedly violated and that the machines possessed no identification or nationality markings. Too many of them had been seen for it to be a fantasy, but their origin was unknown and there appeared to be no obvious reason why their airspace was seeing so many strange and unidentified aircraft passing through it.

The Swedish General Staff catalogued a total of 487 reports of ghost flights and the Finnish General Staff recorded 111.

There was extensive co-operation between Norway, Sweden and Finland and information was freely shared between them, but in spite of all their efforts the identity of the intruders remained a mystery.

There followed a lull of two years and then in 1936 the ghost fliers were seen again, taking the same route as before. They came from the far north – the polar regions – and flew over Norway and then Sweden before returning in the direction from which they had come.[4]

It seems more than likely that at least some of the reports of mystery aircraft were valid, particularly in those cases where the planes had been flying at a low altitude. But why the flights were accompanied by bright lights is something of a mystery. They could be seen as a navigational aid if the plane was flying close to the ground, but why would they be displayed when the aircraft was high in the sky? It is possible, though, that not all sightings of aircraft lights can be relied upon, as according to the press more than 50 per cent of the reports were made between 5 p.m. and 7 p.m., when Venus was low over the horizon.

Phantom plane circles New York

Scandinavia saw an intense and continuous wave of ghost aircraft but similar phenomena were reported further afield. An extraordinary event took place in the middle of New York City on Boxing Day 1933, when a plane was observed circling Manhattan. There was a fierce blizzard at the time and because of it all flights had been cancelled. Thinking that a pilot was in trouble, every airport in New York turned on its landing lights, hoping that it would assist the mystery plane to land, but no attempt was made to touch down. Instead, hundreds of New Yorkers heard the plane circling above the city for several hours and the police department was swamped by people ringing in to report a plane flying at extremely low altitude.

There were no reports of any crashes and no aircraft were reported missing. Who was flying the plane, or why, and what happened to it remains a baffling mystery. Attempts to contact the aircraft by radio proved unsuccessful and whatever phantom aircraft was in the skies that night was never discovered or identified.

What lay behind the extraordinary events in New York City will probably never be accounted for. Mass hysteria is the most common explanation, but with such a volume of witnesses reporting the phantom plane that seems hard to accept as a credible theory.[5]

Mystery aircraft over London

On 1 February 1934, a similar phantom plane was said to have circled London for two hours. The sighting was reported in *The Times*, with the newspaper stating that it appeared to be a large aircraft flying at low altitude and that its course could be traced by its lights. In the light of this report the Air Ministry made enquiries but was unable to find any evidence of an unidentified aircraft. Four days later questions were asked in the House of Commons about the matter and the Under-Secretary of State for Air gave this official explanation:

> The aircraft to which my hon. friend evidently refers was a Royal Air Force aircraft carrying out a training exercise in co-operation with ground forces. Such training flights are arranged in the Royal Air Force without reference to the Air Ministry.

Then on 11 June 1934 two unidentified aircraft were observed circling low over London late at night. They were heard as well as seen and once again *The Times* carried a report on the event. The Air Ministry immediately stated:

> Although night flying was frequently practised
> by RAF machines, and several were up last night,
> service pilots were forbidden by regulations to fly
> over London at less than 5,000 ft. The identity of
> the machine in question was not officially known.[6]

In the climate of 1934 and particularly 1936, the likely culprits for the Scandinavian sightings were considered to be either Germany or the Soviet Union, though both denied involvement in the phenomenon. The suggestion that Japanese aircraft were operating as far away from home as Scandinavia is implausible both in terms of distance and the fact that both Germany and the Soviet Union were far more advanced in terms of aircraft production than Japan. The most likely explanation of these mysterious ghost aircraft involved Nazi or Russian secret programmes to test advanced flying machines.

This is quite reasonable in relation to Scandinavia, but it is a less likely explanation for the London sightings and it is certainly out of the question as far as the New York Boxing Day mystery plane is concerned. The London sightings may well have been secret RAF flights that the government preferred not to acknowledge officially.

Germany jets into the lead

Aviation was a major aspect of German plans to regenerate the country and there is no question that the German aerospace industry was one of the most advanced in the world. With the huge resources pumped into aviation by the Nazis, it is highly probable that the majority of these ghost aircraft were secret German missions. The need for secrecy – because it was illegal for Germany to possess an air force under the Treaty of Versailles – would explain the lack of identification insignia or nationality markings on the aircraft and the fact that the main wave of sightings took place between 1933 and 1934. The description given by witnesses who saw them flying, and in two cases landing, clearly refers to flying boats or seaplanes rather than any kind of circular or saucer type of craft as has sometimes been claimed.

In spite of being hampered by the Treaty of Versailles restrictions, Germany still managed to lead the world in the development of jet aircraft and on 27 August 1939 the Heinkel He 178 made the first-ever flight by a jet plane. The Heinkel He 280, the first turbo-jet powered fighter aircraft in the world, was next on the scene, making its three-minute maiden flight on 30 March 1941, but engine problems and other factors meant that it quickly fell out of favour. Only nine of these aircraft were built and the Luftwaffe then lost confidence in the plane, which was eventually abandoned in favour of the Messerschmitt Me 262.[7]

The Me 262 was 100 mph (161 kph) faster than any Allied aircraft and its four 30 mm (1.18 in) guns gave it enormous firepower. It could have played a decisive part in re-establishing German air superiority, but three main factors prevented that from happening. The first was a marked suspicion by the Luftwaffe of its revolutionary design.

An additional problem was that Hitler and Goering were both obsessed with the idea of building bombers to pummel the opposition into surrender. When Goering saw the Me 262 in Augsburg on 2 November 1943, he immediately demanded to know how many bombs the plane could carry and a short while later Hitler revealed that his thoughts ran in the same direction, by suddenly asking: 'Can this plane also carry bombs?' On 26 November 1943, Hitler was shown the plane at an airshow at Insterburg and he gave orders that it should be deployed as a bomber. 'In this aircraft, which you tell me is a fighter, I see the

Nicknamed the 'swallow' or 'storm bird', the Messerschmitt Me 262 was the world's first operational jet-powered fighter. Introduced in July 1944, it was faster than anything else in the air, but Hitler's aggressive personality meant he wanted it used as a bomber for revenge attacks, rather than taking on the role it was suited for – defensive interceptor.

Blitzbomber with which I will repulse the invasion in its initial and weakest phase.'

In spite of the fact that such a thing was totally impractical, Willy Messerschmitt did not attempt to disillusion Hitler. No one was prepared to argue with the Führer at that stage.

The final difficulty was that the fighter was not produced in sufficiently large numbers, with military priority increasingly being given to heavy bombers and the rocket programmes.

The Me 262 showed its worth during its brief career in combat, with only 300 planes downing over 100 Allied aircraft. But even though it was available for use from 1941, it was both underused and misused – effective deployment of this superb jet fighter from the earliest possible time could have dramatically altered the balance of power in the air. It was vastly superior to any equivalent Allied plane and it would certainly have presented huge problems for the enemy had it been available early enough and in sufficient quantities. Once more a superb design was unable to play its full part because of the unfavourable course of the war.[8]

Reducing drag

One of the key problems with powered flight is overcoming the limitations on speed and manoeuvrability imposed by the 'boundary layer'. This is the very thin layer of air flowing across the surface of the wings of a plane, often only a few molecules thick, which can either be laminar (layered) or turbulent. The ideal situation is laminar flow, in which air flows smoothly and without interruption over the surface of the wing. However, as the boundary layer moves towards the centre of the wing, it is often slowed down by drag and then it becomes turbulent, constraining the speed of the aircraft and reducing lift, particularly at high altitudes. Overcoming these limitations enables the aircraft to fly faster and be more manoeuvrable. Ludwig Prandtl, a German engineer, formulated the concept of the boundary layer at Göttingen University in 1904 and became one of the leading experts on that problem and in aeronautical engineering generally.[9]

Swept wing aircraft were an early attempt by German aeronautical engineers to reduce drag. It was found that air passing over wings set at an angle would inhibit boundary layer formation. Their pioneering research in the field led to the Me 163 Komet, introduced in 1944, which was the only operational rocket-powered aircraft, and the jet-powered Me 262, both of which were fitted with swept wings that dramatically improved their speed and manoeuvrability.[10]

Glider development was one means of studying and resolving aeronautical problems, as gliders do not have the benefit of engine power to create airflow and lift. Werner Pfenninger was one of the leading designers of gliders and sailplanes and in 1938 he produced the *Elfe 1*, which flew in early 1939. It was exceptionally manoeuvrable, stable and fast and had a low sinking speed. He worked particularly hard on the wing profiles. The *Elfe 1* had a very small wingspan and a highly efficient rudder and ailerons, but in spite of the small wingspan it was so aerodynamically streamlined that it achieved maximum lift. The gap between the wing and the aileron meant that airflow over the aileron could be reduced. To increase speed, the ailerons could be raised by four degrees. Pfenninger followed the *Elfe 1* with the *Elfe 2* in 1944, which had a wider wingspan and a heavier weight.[11]

In 1944 Pfenninger was asked to produce a laminar flow sailplane for the Horten brothers, who were themselves exceptional aeronautical engineers. Among other aircraft they had produced the Horten H-IV, a tailless flying wing glider, four of which were constructed between 1941 and 1943. They had even designed the first 'stealth' aircraft. Pfenninger's Horten 4B glider, which employed a laminar flow profile as the brothers

Crowds gather around a Messerschmitt Me 163 at the Wright-Patterson Air Force Museum, Ohio, c. 1968. In the top-right-hand corner, you can see a tame V-1 rocket.

had requested, was a revolutionary but ultimately unsuccessful design, but after the war he designed the first successful laminar flow sailplane.[12]

Suction wings

Other German scientists pursued another, perhaps more obvious, route. Why not just remove the boundary layer completely? In order to achieve their aim, they devoted considerable effort towards the development of suction wings. They believed that this system would allow them to either eliminate or reduce dramatically the drag problems created by boundary layer effects.

The first attempts at suction wings involved cutting slots into an aircraft's wings and then using engines to suck the air from the boundary layer and redeploy it into the fuselage. These early experiments failed, primarily through the need to employ multiple engines. One was needed to produce power and a second was necessary to extract and circulate the air.[13]

Two suction wing aircraft were then built; the Junkers AF-1 *Absaugegeflug* (suction aircraft) and the Fieseler AF-2 *Absaugegestorch* (suction stork). Pfenninger was brought in at this stage and became involved in attempts to use multiple slots to create continuous suction, but he was unable to achieve satisfactory results.[14]

The problems of pure suction led to new research into a combined system where both suction and blowing were used to reduce drag and improve performance. This concept was put into practice by the Arado and Dornier companies, who both made bombers – the AR-23/A and the Do 20-24 – which were STOL (short take-off and landing) aircraft. These planes 'sucked' the boundary layer through slots on the ailerons and then blew the air on to the ailerons by using a pump in the wing.[15]

German aerospace engineers worked on many unorthodox approaches to aviation. One plane combined a radical new design with an attempt to use the principle of suction to achieve greater speed. This aircraft, the Junkers AF-1 *Absauge Flugzeug*, a high-winged light monoplane which used 'suction wings' to increase the lift of the aircraft,[16] may have been the first plane to break the sound barrier. At the *Aerodynamische Versuchsanstalt* (AVA) in Göttingen, a number of scientists and engineers conducted a test flight of the AF-1 in 1937.

A new model known as the AF-2 was devised in 1940 and by 1942 it was able to fly at almost the maximum possible lift factor. A greater degree of lift was certainly possible compared with other planes, but it was a slow aircraft and therefore vulnerable to attack.

Research on both improving aerofoil properties and the force of the suction continued. Wind tunnel tests were conducted while using the compressor in an aircraft as a suction pump and it was found that it improved aerodynamic resistance. By 1944, this research had reached the stage where blueprints were drawn up for a suction wing supersonic jet fighter.

There is no definite proof that these planes got beyond the design stage except for some strange stories in 1944 about fighters 'moving through the air like a sponge through water and completely different from everything ever seen'. These accounts came from France and were generally assumed to refer to some kind of improved version of the V-2 rocket. What we know is that the British Miles Aircraft company also worked on suction wing technology and that their design was almost identical to the AF-1. Miles managed to reduce aerodynamic resistance by over 20 per cent but ran into technical problems and abandoned the project.[17]

Another possible candidate for breaking the sound barrier was the Lippisch P-13a, designed by Professor Alexander Lippisch, who led the world in ramjet research. After first designing the P-12 aircraft he went on to create the improved P-13a version in May 1944. The delta-winged P-13a was designed as a supersonic fighter and somewhat amazingly Lippisch decided to power it with a ramjet engine that used granule-sized coal as a fuel. The plane was completed by January 1945 after successful wind tunnel testing.

This aircraft reached a top speed of 1,200 mph (1,931 kph) and according to Polish records made successful test flights in January and February 1945. American records indicate that it was captured by the Allies and may well have been the basis on which one of their own pilots was subsequently able to break the sound barrier. Lippisch was certainly recruited by the Americans and worked on a number of projects for them while employed by Convair, so he was the designer most likely to have been able to accomplish this feat.[18]

Fireballs

While some German aeronautical engineers were working on new and improved planes, others were dreaming up different types of flying weapons. Some of these seemed to have come straight from the pages of a science fiction novel. One of those was the *Feuerball* (Fireball), which arose out of research into the possibility of interfering with the engine systems of enemy aircraft. It was designed to produce electromagnetic fields of sufficient intensity to short-circuit a plane's ignition and thereby force it to crash.

The earliest *Feuerball* versions were simply silver jet-powered discs. They were launched by catapults and then remotely controlled by ground operators. An added refinement was the fact that they were fitted with klystron tubes that jammed Allied radar and allowed them to engage with enemy aircraft without being detected on their systems.[19] A witness to the test flights said: 'During the day it looked like a shining disc spinning on its axis and during the night it looked like a burning globe.'

Later *Feuerballs* were circular in shape and resembled the shell of a tortoise. They were devised to be controlled by radio and then on take-off to follow the exhaust trails of enemy

Alexander Lippisch became fascinated with flight when he witnessed a demonstration by Orville Wright over Tempelhof Field, Berlin in 1909. He became a pioneer of aerodynamics, specializing in flying wings, delta wings and the ground effect. Perhaps his most famous design was the Me 163.

planes. In operation, they produced a large surrounding corona of luminous flames which led to their code name of *Feuerball*. Their purpose was to incapacitate the radar equipment of the enemy aircraft.

The high degree of ionization achieved by the *Feuerball* meant that in spite of its visibility it was almost undetectable by radar. Its lack of direct combat capability also meant that Allied fighters did not fire upon the balls of fire, fearing that an explosion might result if they did. Many pilots imagined that these devices could be detonated by German ground staff to bring their planes down. This fear was partly justified as the *Feuerballs* did contain a high-explosive charge within them that would destroy them in flight if there was damage to the guidance system. In spite of that, one American pilot tried to shoot down a *Feuerball* but was unable to hit it.[20]

A ground equivalent of the *Feuerball* was the *Feuermolch* (Fire Salamander), at least 50 of which were used by the Germans in France as they were gradually expelled from the country. It operated on the same principle as the *Feuerball* but was operated from the ground on the same basis as artillery. The *Feuerland* (Fire Land) was also devised and was intended to jam radio communications, but it was not developed in time to be used by the Wehrmacht.

Towards the end of the war both the *Feuerland* and the *Feuermolch* devices were destroyed to prevent them from falling into Allied hands.[21]

By 1942 the AEG company had taken the *Feuerball* concept further by developing *Kugelwaffen* (Ball Weapons). These were ceramic objects in the shape of bells, using plasma engines. Until 1944 they were unarmed but following D-Day they were used to attack enemy planes. The *Kugelwaffen* shut down the radar and engine systems of Allied aircraft and their appearance caused consternation.

Work on further development of the *Feuerball* project was accelerated in late 1944, under the auspices of the OBF centre for aviation research, but in spite of extensive attempts to improve on the design the work had not been successfully completed when the war ended. However, Albert Speer took up a modified version of the idea and scientists under his control attempted to develop 'proximity radio interference' systems. These were designed to impact on the electronic apparatus of night fighters.

If the existence of the *Feuerball* stretches the imagination, its successor, the Zeppelin Werk *Kugelblitz* (Ball Lightning), ventures into UFO territory. Some commentators have even called it a flying saucer. It was described as an unmanned jet lift aircraft with a circular shape that fused the wings, fuselage and tail into a single body. In addition, it incorporated a variety of revolutionary aeronautical features such as gyroscopic stabilization, vertical take-off and landing, an anti-radar force, an infrared searching function, an electrostatically fired weapon system, an explosive aerosol gun and even television guidance.

It is said that on its one and only combat mission the *Kugelblitz* destroyed a whole squadron of US B-24 bombers over Lake Garda. Its aerosol gun caused havoc and the result of this operation was to spread panic among Allied aircrews. In spite of its proven success, the weapon was destroyed in April 1945 to prevent it from falling into enemy hands.[22]

Taking the circular route

Circular wing aircraft design looked outwardly more straightforward than the *Feuerball* project, but while the advantages of circular-winged flight were clear – they included vertical take-off and aerodynamic efficiency – ultimate success was tantalizingly just out of reach. Alexander Lippisch was one of the engineers who took up the challenge and from

1941 onwards he worked on circular wing experiments for Messerschmitt, subjecting his design to wind tunnel testing at Göttingen. He later worked on a *Drehflügel* (rotating wing), which was tested at Peenemünde. However, these projects, which were at the cutting edge of aeronautical research, were still not fully developed by the time the war ended.[23]

Such was the thirst for new ideas in Nazi Germany that they were eagerly seized upon, no matter how unlikely the source. Arthur Sack, for instance, was not an aeronautical engineer but a German farmer from near Leipzig, whose hobby was building and flying model aircraft. In July 1939 'The First Reich-wide Contest for Motorized Flying Models' was held in Leipzig. What was unusual about Sack's entry to the competition was its circular wing. Most of the competitors were unable even to launch their model craft and Sack was no exception. Finally, in desperation at its failure to lift off through his guidance system, he picked it up and threw it into the air. It managed to travel 100 m (328 ft) and was just able to reach the finishing line.

Nothing more might have been heard of Sack and his model if an important guest had not been watching the proceedings. Ernst Udet, chief of armaments procurement for the Luftwaffe, had observed Sack's entry with considerable interest. In spite of the poor performance of Sack's model, Udet had been impressed by its potential. The two aspects that appealed to him were its STOL (short take-off and landing) capabilities and its circular wings. Udet knew that a design of that type could reduce drag and improve aircraft speed and the result was that he commissioned Sack to build improved versions of his AS-1 for use by the Luftwaffe.

Sack began working on the AS series in association with MiMo (*Mitteldeutsche Motoren Werke* – Middle German Motor Works), a firm of aircraft subcontractors based at Brandis airfield near Leipzig. The airfield had large runways and was frequently used by the Luftwaffe for test flights as well as serving as a base for fighter aircraft. He worked hard on a series of models and each one represented an improvement on its predecessor. Once the AS-5 had flown successfully, Sack felt confident enough in the soundness of his design to create a full-sized aircraft to be test flown.

Work on the AS 6.V-1 began in January 1944. The frame was made from plywood and the cockpit and landing gear were scavenged from a crashed Me Bf 109B. Even the engine was cannibalized from an Me Bf 108 Taifun.

By February Sack was ready to embark on a test flight. The result was complete failure. It was obvious that the rudder was too weak and the engine was too low-powered to provide sufficient lift and thrust. The plane also suffered structural damage during the trials.

Subsequent testing revealed further problems with the aircraft. The control surfaces were placed in the circular wing, which

The Drehflügel *was an eccentric, helicopterish contraption with rotating wings that never quite got off the ground; it was probably based on a model like this.*

meant that while the plane was taxiing the vacuum created by the wing prevented the controls from functioning. On the last of the five tests, the right leg of the landing gear was damaged.

The most fundamental problem of all was the underpowered engine. In an attempt to correct this problem, the angle of incidence was increased. The test pilot proposed moving the landing gear, but this would have required too many modifications and his suggestion was rejected. A makeshift remedy was applied instead, which involved increasing the tail surfaces and adding brakes from a Junkers Ju-88. None of these changes improved the plane's performance, however, and on its next test flight the AS 6.V-1 simply rolled and eventually made a short hop but could not become airborne.

The next test flight saw the aircraft make a longer jump before banking sharply to the left. Again, the defective engine was the root of the problem, but because of the increasing constraints on supply and the low priority given to the AS 6.V-1 project an improved engine was not installed.

Sack's aircraft stagnated at Brandis until the summer of 1944, when the elite fighter group 1/JG400 arrived. These were experienced and confident pilots who were well used to flying STOL aircraft and other experimental planes. Franz Rössle volunteered to fly what he and his comrades nicknamed the *Bierdecke* (Beer Tray), but for all his skill as a pilot his attempts to fly the AS 6.V-1 ended with only a slight powered hop followed by a crash and damaged landing gear. He suggested handing over the whole project to Messerschmitt so they could fit it with new components, but Sack refused to give up control of his project to Messerschmitt so no further testing or development took place. As a result of his experiences Rössle gave the plane a new nickname – the *Bussard* (Buzzard) – because it spent most of its time on the ground and was made up of scavenged parts from other aircraft.

Rössle's account of the plane led Messerschmitt to formulate the idea of the Me-600. This would have employed a far larger circular wing and would also have been fitted with advanced Messerschmitt engines, improved landing gear and control system and six guns in the circular wing. The project was considered but not even a prototype was built. Later Allied bombing raids damaged the AS 6.V-1 beyond repair. As troops began to close in on the site the wreckage of Sack's plane was destroyed by the Germans themselves.[24]

At the beginning of the 21st century a version of the AS 6.V-1 was built by enthusiasts in Australia. It had a better engine and better control systems and flew successfully.[25]

FOOTNOTES

1 Ralph Barker, *The Schneider Trophy Races*, Airlife Publishing, 1981

2 Jacques Vallée, *UFOs in Space: Anatomy of a Phenomenon*, Ballantine, 1987

3 http://www.cagliostro.se/2011/05/02/the-ghost-fliers-2775134/

4 Vallée, op. cit.

5 Timothy Good, *Above Top Secret: The Worldwide UFO Cover-up*, Sidgwick and Jackson, 1987

6 Ibid.

7 H. Dieter Koehler, *Ernst Heinkel: Pionier der Schnellflugzeuge*, Bernard and Graefe, 1999

8 Colin Heaton, *The Me 262 Stormbird: From the Pilots Who Flew, Fought and Survived It*, Zenith, 2012

9 Johanna Vogel-Prandtl, *Ludwig Prandtl: A Personal Biography Drawn from Memories and Correspondence*, Universitätsverlag Göttingen, 2014

10 Jeffrey L. Ethell, *Komet, The Messerschmitt 163*, Ian Allan, 1978

11 Albert L. Braslow, *A History of Suction-Type Laminar-Flow Control with Emphasis on Flight Research*, NASA, 1999

12 Russell E. Lee, *Only the Wing: Reimar Horten's Epic Quest to Stabilize and Control the All-Wing Aircraft*, Smithsonian, 2012

13 Joseph P. Farrell, op. cit.

14 Ibid.

15 Richard P. Bateson, *Arado Ar 234 Blitz (Aircraft Profile 215)*, Profile Publications, 1972; Peter de Jong, *Dornier Do 24 Units (Osprey Combat Aircraft No 110)*, Osprey Aerospace, 2015

16 Farrell, op. cit.

17 Ibid.

18 Ibid.

19 Renato Vesco and David Hatcher-Childress, *Man-Made UFOs 1944–1994: 50 Years of Suppression*, Adventures Unlimited, 1994

20 Ibid.

21 Ibid.

22 Ibid.

23 Henry Stevens, *Hitler's Flying Saucers: A Guide to German Flying Discs of the Second World War*, Adventures Unlimited, 2014

24 J. Miranda and P. Mercado, *Flugzeug Profile 23 – Deutsche Kreisflügelflugzeuge*, Flugzeug Publikations GmbH, 1995

25 Rob Arndt, 'Arthur Sack AS6/Me 600 Bussard (1939–1945)', http://discaircraft.greyfalcon.us/ARTHUR%20SACK%20A.htm/

CHAPTER THREE

ROCKET DEVELOPMENT

Rocket pioneer

The history of modern rocketry began at the turn of the 20th century. Their first use was by scientists attempting to prevent hailstorms by firing rockets into the clouds and exploding them, but in the process both the rockets and the hailstorms disintegrated.

If he is to be believed, Pedro Paulet went much further than shooting rockets into clouds. The Peruvian inventor claimed that in 1895 he had built a liquid-fuel rocket engine and five years later had developed a rocket propulsion system. He also claimed to have designed reaction motors in 1895 and to have built an aircraft using rocket engines and thermoelectric batteries in 1902.

Paulet also stated that nuclear-propelled rockets could be built to fly to the moon. In spite of his claims to have designed and tested rockets at an early stage, it was not until 1927 that he wrote a letter to the Peruvian newspaper *El Comercio* declaring that he had first achieved this feat.

German engineer Alfred Maul attached cameras to rockets in 1906 in order to photograph the ground from the air, making an early attempt at aerial reconnaissance. However, his pioneering idea was abandoned as aircraft developed.[1]

Paulet had his followers, though. Alexander Scherschevsky, an assistant to the German rocket pioneer Hermann Oberth, was convinced of the truth of Paulet's claims. Another who believed them was Willy Ley, one of the great names in rocketry and space travel. Even Wernher von Braun described Paulet as 'one of the fathers of aeronautics' and 'the pioneer of the liquid fuel propulsion motor'.[2] He declared that 'by his efforts, Paulet helped man reach the Moon'.[3] Other experts in the field were less convinced by Paulet's claims and Paulet himself never declared that his rockets had flown.

Paulet is said to have invented his rocket motor while he was a student at the Sorbonne University in France. He experimented with an engine made from vanadium steel and fuelled by a mixture of nitrogen peroxide and petrol. There is no doubt that the members of the VfR (*Verein für Raumschiffahrt* – Society for Space Travel) regarded Paulet as a serious researcher and many of their books and magazines from the late 1920s make considerable reference to his work. Contemporary Soviet scientists were also aware of him and made use of his researches. If his claims were true, it makes him the first person to successfully design a liquid-fuelled rocket engine, nearly 30 years before its acknowledged inventor, Robert Goddard.

Paulet also designed the Girándula propulsion system in 1900. In 1944, he described it as follows:

> It consisted of a bicycle wheel, fitted with three rockets fed by tubes attached to the spokes. The

fuel comes through the tubes from a kind of fixed carburettor, placed near the axis, with a ring of holes. This explosive mixture flows through the tubes, every time the nozzle faces one of the holes. The number of rockets could be increased, until they come to look like a comfortably enclosed turbine.

The results were very encouraging: the wheel turned apparently indefinitely, and although the experiments were, as indicated, highly secret, word of their success reached the Latin Quarter [in Paris], which is perhaps why an English author has referred to me as one of the first driving forces of rocket flight.[4]

Paulet then designed the Avión Torpedo in 1902, an aircraft with thermal walls using resistant materials and supplied with electricity through thermoelectric batteries.

Max Valier, an important name in rocket research and development, said of Paulet in his book *Der Vorstoss in den Weltenraum* (The Advance into Space):

Paulet's work is even more significant for the present project of development of a rocket ship, as they have proven for the first time – as compared to the few seconds of the burning of powder rockets – that it is possible, by the use of liquid fuels, to construct a rocket engine that would burn for an hour.[5]

Paulet was clearly a pioneer in the field of rocketry and it is unsurprising that the Nazis were keen to recruit him to assist their efforts. The German Astronautical Society invited him to Germany to become part of a team of researchers into rocket propulsion and he was initially interested, but when he discovered that the intention was to construct a weapon that would be used for military purposes he declined the invitation. As late as 1965, Oberth described him as one of the true pioneers of rocket science.

Guided missiles

The First World War, not surprisingly, saw a considerable amount of research into military uses for rockets. Some were actually launched but they soon showed themselves to be ineffective compared with the other available artillery weapons. Their main use was either to illuminate battlefields to help troops or to lay 'smoke screens' to act as camouflage for forthcoming military action.

The 'illumination' technique used rockets that exploded in brilliant flashes of light, giving a clear view of a battlefield for a few seconds. Some rockets were equipped with parachutes that had a flare attached to them. As the parachute descended, it lit up the battleground for around 30 seconds.

Different nations attempted to add rockets to their armoury. For instance, the French tried using Le Prieur rockets, which were strictly designed for air-to-air combat, against German observation balloons. They were reasonably successful but they did not perform as well as other artillery weapons and they had a very limited range.[6]

The British developed the first guided missile, which was known as the A.T. (Aerial Target). This project was set up at the beginning of the war and the research was supervised by Professor A. M. Low. His idea was to design a small pilotless monoplane that could be remotely controlled by radio and then fill it full of explosives. The aim was that the radio signals would be able to guide the bombs to their target. Power would be supplied by a 35-horsepower Granville Bradshaw engine. The name A.T. was chosen in the hope of misleading the Germans into believing that the planes were drones intended to test the effectiveness of anti-aircraft artillery, rather than weapons with an offensive capability.

Two test flights took place in March 1917 at the Royal Flying Corps training field at Upavon, Wiltshire. Both vehicles crashed when the engines failed but in spite of that failure the tests demonstrated that it was possible to direct rockets through the use of radio signals.[7]

The A.T. project was cancelled but the United States then came up with their version of a remotely powered missile. At the request of the United States army, the Delco and Sperry companies began to develop the Kettering Aerial Torpedo (later known as the 'Kettering Bug') under the supervision of Charles Kettering. This was a biplane bomber constructed of wood with a total weight of 600 lb (272 kg), which would be powered by a 40-hp Ford engine. The weight of the plane included a 300 lb (136 kg) bomb payload.

After the engineers had determined wind speed, the distance of the target and wind direction, they calculated how many revolutions of the engine would be necessary to direct the missile to its intended destination. Once this figure had been reached a cam dropped into position and the 'Bug' took off. It was launched by a four-wheeled carriage running along a portable track, similar to the method that had been used by the Wright brothers. Once airborne a gyroscope was used to control the vehicle and an aneroid barometer measured its altitude. When it reached its objective, the wings on the plane detached themselves and the fuselage carrying its bomb load landed on the target. The Kettering Bug demonstrated its capabilities to Army Air Corps observers in Dayton, Ohio in 1918 and would almost certainly have gone into full production but for the end of the First World War.[8]

The British then came back into the equation. Having made significant progress during the First World War, British researchers became involved in further projects. In 1927, they tested a missile known as the Larynx at the Royal Aircraft Establishment. The Larynx was a monoplane with radio guidance that was flight tested from HMS *Stronghold* at sea and at a test ground in Egypt. It could carry a 250 lb (113 kg) bomb at a speed of 200 mph (322 kph) and hit a target that lay 100 miles (161 km) distant.

Then in 1930 British engineers produced two biplanes guided by radio and launched by a catapult, either from ships or from ground bases. They called them the Queen Bee and the Queen Wasp. Both missiles could drop a high-explosive charge and return home to their launch pad.[9]

Rocket research around the world

In the 1920s and 1930s, there was a resurgence of interest in rocket technology. Research was not only conducted by governments but also by members of the rocket societies that sprang up worldwide. Rockets seemed to be the way forward and actual and potential uses for them ranged from military weapons to interplanetary travel, delivering mail and powering cars.

Britain and Russia

In 1935, the British began carrying out rocket tests at Woolwich Arsenal. They used smokeless cordite as the fuel and the intention was primarily to develop anti-aircraft rockets. The possible use of rockets as long-range attack weapons was also investigated. A series of small two- or three-inch charges were used in rockets, some tested in clusters, and by 1939 rockets were sufficiently developed to become a small part of British weaponry. The navy used them to defend ships from hostile aircraft.[10]

Russian scientists, particularly after the triumph of the Bolsheviks, became involved in considerable research into the possibilities of rockets. In this they were aided by Konstantin Tsiolkovsky, who was one of the leading scientific experts in the field of rocketry. His fascination with spaceflight came about through reading Jules Verne's novels and in 1895 the newly constructed Eiffel Tower inspired him to formulate the idea of the space elevator. His theoretical analysis became the foundation for subsequent research and development in Russia and his 1903 work *The Exploration of Cosmic Space by Means of Reaction Devices* is one of the pioneering treatises on space travel.[11]

Tsiolkovsky became disillusioned with the lack of enthusiasm for his projects, however, and by the time the First World War had broken out he had abandoned rocketry. Although he strongly supported the Bolshevik Revolution in 1917, he played little active part in the subsequent development of rockets.

The Soviet government set up two new organizations in 1924 – the Central Bureau for the Study of the Problems of Rockets and the All-Union Society for the Study of Interplanetary Flight – and gave them a twofold brief. They were to consider the possibility of spaceflight and the military application of rocket technology.

In 1930, the government began testing the possibilities of rockets. Fridrikh Tsander and Valentin Glushko led the design teams and trialled liquid-fuelled rocket engines. Both men made their findings available by writing books on the subject, Tsander producing *Problems of Flight by Means of Reactive Devices* in 1932 and Glushko publishing *Rockets, Their Construction and Utilization* in 1935.

These Russian rocket tests showed considerable promise and a variety of fuel combinations were tried, including mixtures of petrol and gaseous air, petrol and liquid oxygen, kerosene and nitric acid, kerosene and tetranitromethane and toluene with nitrogen tetroxide.

One of the most significant rockets to be developed through these tests was the GIRD-X, which was 8 ft 6 in (2.59 m) long and 6 in (15 cm) wide and weighed 65 lb (29.5 kg). During a test launch on 25 November 1933, it attained an altitude of 3 miles (4.83 km). In 1936, another Russian rocket known as the *Aviavnito*, weighing 213 lb (96.6 kg) and 10 ft long by 1 ft wide (3.05 x 0.3 m), attained an altitude of 3.5 miles (5.63 km).[12]

Italy

The Italians began rocket research in 1929, designing engines burning different types of fuel, including trinitroglycerin and nitromethane, trinitroglycerin and methyl alcohol and petrol with nitrogen dioxide. The tests were promising but with restricted funding no rockets were produced. In 1935, the Italians abandoned all further research into rocketry.

United States

The American inventor Robert Goddard is largely responsible for the birth of rocket science in America. He made huge theoretical contributions as well as developing and launching rockets to demonstrate their potential. Like von Braun, Goddard was motivated by the dream of space travel and he hoped to be able to send a rocket to the moon and eventually further into space. He raised some financial backing from the Smithsonian Institution and between 1920 and 1926 designed, built and launched the first rocket powered by liquid fuel: a mixture of liquid oxygen and petrol. On 16 March 1926, his rocket made its maiden test flight at his aunt's farm at Auburn, Massachusetts and in 1929 he successfully sent a barometer, a camera and a thermometer up in a rocket flight.[13]

The American flier Charles Lindbergh heard of Goddard's experiments and organized a petition to the Daniel Guggenheim Foundation Fund for the Promotion of Aeronautics, calling for further funding. This allowed Goddard to employ assistants and he then designed rockets that reached higher altitudes.[14]

In January 1932, the American Interplanetary Society (AIS), one of the rocket societies that sprang up at that time, also began designing a liquid-fuel rocket. It was modelled on the pattern of the VfR rockets and burned a mixture of petrol and liquid oxygen, which was enclosed in an aluminium alloy framework. Construction of AIS Rocket 1, as it was known, began in August 1932 at a farm in Stockton, New Jersey, and by 12 November of that year a static test launch produced a thrust of 60 lb (27.2 kg). In spite of further development, the rocket was never test flown. A variant, the Rocket 2, was launched on 14 May 1933 from Staten Island, but its oxygen tank burst when it reached 250 ft (76.2 m). Tests for new developments of the model were planned but only one was ever launched. All testing stopped with the coming of the Second World War.

In 1936 the Americans made an attempt at producing rocket-powered planes. Two 15 ft (4.57 m) aircraft were launched from an iced-over lake in New York, both being powered by a rocket engine burning a mixture of alcohol and liquid oxygen. One plane crashed after only fifteen seconds when its wings were torn off and the other climbed to 1,000 ft (305 m) before running out of fuel. Willy Ley, by now a defector to the United States, was in charge of the project. In the same year experiments with liquid-fuelled rockets began for the US navy. Several prototypes were built which burned a mixture of petrol and compressed air. They showed promise but no real emphasis was placed on their development and the US lost the chance to lead the world in rocket research.

The American military made little attempt to develop rocketry and though occasional tests took place to try and develop missiles they failed to create an accurate aerial weapon and further research was abandoned. It is surprising that the

Americans failed to build upon Goddard's knowledge and expertise, which could have enabled them to become the pioneers of rocketry, rather than the Germans. Even during the course of the war they concentrated on conventional weapons and the atomic bomb, rather than on developing rocketry.[15]

VfR

The *Verein für Raumschiffahrt* was a German amateur rocket association with around 500 members, some of whom were, or went on to become, highly influential figures in the field of rocketry. Its members conducted a series of experiments and test firings, some relatively successful, and a significant amount of development work on liquid-fuelled rockets was carried out.

The VfR was formed in Breslau on 5 June 1927 by Johannes Winkler. Other co-founders were Max Valier and Willy Ley, who had been called in by the German director Fritz Lang as 'expert advisers' on his science fiction film *Frau im Mond* (The Woman in the Moon). One of its members, Hermann Oberth, was the leading German expert on rocketry and his influence was as great in Germany as Tsiolkovsky's was in Russia. Oberth's classic book *Die Rakete zu den Planetenräumen* (The Rocket into Interplanetary Space) became the bible for future rocket research and development.

Another key player in the VfR was Walter Hohmann, who was also the author of a definitive work, *Die Erreichbarkeit der Himmelskörper* (The Attainability of Celestial Bodies). This was such an exceptional contribution to rocket science that it was consulted by NASA during their own projects for space exploration.

Ley and Oberth hoped to persuade Lang to fund the launch of a rocket to coincide with the release of his film but they were unsuccessful. Valier had been able to obtain financial support from Fritz Opel for rocket-powered stunts that were designed to gain publicity for the Opel company, but Lang was unable to provide the necessary funding for the rocket launch.

The society attracted many young scientists and soon began designing and building rockets. At this stage, the principal motivation was the desire to explore space and try to create craft capable of interplanetary travel. One of the youngest members of the VfR was a 17-year-old scientist named Wernher von Braun, who had been obsessed from an early age with the dream of spaceflight. Like many others he too had been inspired by Oberth's *Die Rakete zu den Planetenräumen*. After he arrived unannounced at Willy Ley's home and asked to join the VfR, Ley introduced him to Oberth, who asked him to raise funds for the society. His first job was standing in front of a display of model rockets in Wertheim's department store in Berlin, while attempting to persuade German housewives that in their lifetime humans would walk on the Moon. Ironically, the store was being picketed at the time by Nazi stormtroopers, who were holding up placards advising shoppers not to buy from Jews.

The display, and von Braun's part in it, was part of a publicity drive for Fritz Lang's film. It was during this film that Oberth invented the 'countdown' for rocket launches. Before long the VfR published a journal, *Die Rakete* (The Rocket), which flourished between 1927 and 1929, and in 1928 Ley published a classic work, *Die Möglichkeit der Weltraumfahrt* (The Possibility of Space Travel).[16]

The VfR contacted the Wehrmacht, the German army, for funding in September 1930. This was well before the Nazis came to power and when the Weimar Republic, though struggling with the Depression, still seemed likely to survive. The Treaty of Versailles in 1919 had forbidden Germany to possess an air force and had greatly restricted its military capability, but rockets had not been banned. In the light of that loophole, the VfR was given permission to build and test rockets.

These tests were originally supervised by another team member, Klaus Riedel, who was killed in a car accident late in the war. They took place at an empty munitions dump in Reinickendorf, near Berlin, which was nicknamed *Raketenflugplatz* (Rocket Airfield) by the crew.[17] The first rocket to be tested was called the *Mirak-1* (Minimum Rocket 1). It was fuelled with a mixture of petrol and liquid oxygen, a twelve-inch liquid oxygen tank served as a cooling agent for the combustion chamber and a three-foot long tail stick carried the petrol. The first test of the *Mirak-1* took place in August 1930 at Bernstadt in Saxony and was pronounced a success. The second test in September 1930 was a failure as the liquid oxygen tank burst and *Mirak-1* exploded.

In the spring of 1931, the *Mirak-2* was tested. Its design was similar to its predecessor, but the propulsion system was superior. However, it was destroyed during testing when, as with the previous model, its liquid oxygen tank burst and the rocket exploded.[18]

Ley named the next series of rockets the *Repulsor*. Like its predecessor, the *Repulsor* burned a combination fuel: a mixture of petrol and liquid oxygen. The process for cooling the combustion chamber was different, though, with water stored within an aluminium skin carrying out the cooling. The *Repulsor* was much more successful than its predecessors, reaching altitudes of over 1,000 m (3,280 ft). This achievement led to Captain Walter Dornberger and two other Wehrmacht officers attending a test launch in the spring of 1932. The launch was a failure, but Dornberger was so impressed by the rocket's potential that he issued a contract for a further demonstration.

Dornberger soon noticed the exceptional ability Wernher von Braun displayed in the field. In 1930, von Braun had assisted Hermann Oberth at the University of Berlin in his work on liquid-fuelled rocket testing and he was greatly influenced by him. His chief motivation was the desire to conquer space and he was willing to follow any path that would facilitate that dream, even if it meant working for the Nazis. Before long he would be recruited by the German military to develop the potential of rockets for warfare.

The VfR then disagreed among themselves over this offer by the military. Von Braun wanted them to accept, but the others, fearing that the results of their research would be used by a possible Nazi government, wanted to refuse. In the end, after heated discussion, the VfR rejected the offer of a contract.

With Hitler's appointment as Chancellor in January 1933, these disagreements made it increasingly hard for the VfR to function as an independent group. Von Braun and those

Walter R. Dornberger was a former German artillery officer who led the V-2 programme. Along with other Nazi rocket scientists, he was co-opted into working for the Americans after the war, in his case for the Bell Aircraft Corporation from 1950 to 1960. This was the drawing of a Rocket Airliner he showed to the Institute of Aeronautical Sciences in Chicago; he claimed it would be able to make the 2,600-mile (4,180 km) journey from London to New York in an hour and a quarter at 8,300 mph (13,358 kph).

who were willing to become part of military projects joined the Wehrmacht's rocket programme, but the other members refused to be associated with it. In 1934, refusing to yield to Nazi pressure for assimilation, the VfR dissolved itself. One of the dissident VfR members, Herbert Schaefer, emigrated to America in 1935 and took with him the only known surviving physical evidence of the VfR programme, an aluminium *Repulsor* nozzle, which is now in the Smithsonian Institution.

Bogus spaceflight

Rudolf Nebel was an early and enthusiastic member of the VfR, but he was widely distrusted by the other members for his lack of technical expertise, his volatile temperament and his extreme nationalist politics. In spite of these handicaps, he nearly became the first man to successfully test fly a liquid-fuelled rocket, narrowly losing out to the American rocket pioneer Robert Goddard.

In 1932 he published a work on the subject, *Raketenflug* (Rocket Flight), and the same year saw him become involved in a crazy project devised by Franz Mengering, an engineer who worked for the city of Magdeburg. Mengering was a believer in the absurd 'Hollow Earth' theories of Peter Bender (Goering was also a disciple) and thought that the truth of this theory could be demonstrated through an experiment. He claimed that a rocket fired vertically downwards from the city of Magdeburg would land to the south of New Zealand and he somehow managed to persuade the city council to fund this experiment.

Nebel was given a contract of 25,000 marks so that he could conduct preliminary experiments, but for a rocket that went upwards. He undertook to build a rocket that could carry a man up to 1 km (0.62 miles) above the Earth, after which the pilot would leave the craft and parachute back to safety. Nebel's rocket was based on the *Repulsor* model and was due to be launched on 11 June 1933. By that time, the Nazis were in power and Nebel, a Party member, hoped to find favour with them for his experiments. Unfortunately, the launch was an utter failure, with the rocket managing to climb no higher than 1,000 ft (305 m), and that on its fourth attempt. The authorities, both in Magdeburg and Germany, lost patience with him and he was frozen out of all subsequent work on rocketry while the Third Reich lasted.

Later, a completely false legend grew up that his rocket launch had not only succeeded but had managed to fly into outer space. Nevertheless, Nebel was an important rocket pioneer, although he was never in the same class as Ley, von Braun and the other rocket scientists.[19]

Rocket-powered vehicles

The Germans and the Austrians became so enamoured with rockets that they seemed to want to add them to everything that moved, from cars to sleds.

First off was the German automotive manufacturer Opel, who conducted a number of tests of rocket-powered cars. The first was the Opel-RAK 1, which was tested in 1928. It was a modified racing car which was powered by Sander solid-propellant rockets. Further tests on this device were carried out using six and then eight rockets before the final version was developed, in which 12 Sander rockets were used to propel the car. When it was tested on 12 April 1928, only seven of the 12 rockets fired successfully but the car reached a speed of 70 mph (113 kph).

This was followed by the Opel-RAK 2, which was powered by a battery of 24 Sander rockets and reached a maximum speed of 125 mph (201 kph) when it was tested on 23 May 1928. Opel's main concern was to use rocket technology to achieve faster racing cars and his designs had little impact on the future development of rocketry.

Experiments on rocket-powered railway cars were also carried out, again using Sander rockets. June 1928 saw the first test carried out on a track between Celle and Burgwedel, in which 24 Sander rockets drove a railway car at a speed of 100 mph (161 kph). Further tests were conducted on a railway track between Blankenburg and Halberstadt. These proved unsuccessful, however, with the rockets failing to propel the railway car.

The first rocket-powered aircraft, the *Ente* (Duck), was a glider with two Sander rockets added to it. On 11 June 1928, it flew for three-quarters of a mile (1.2 km) in less than a minute on a test flight conducted by the German glider group Rhön-Rossitten Gesellschaft. Inspired by this feat, Opel flew a glider powered by 16 Sander rockets on 30 September 1928, attaining a speed of 95 mph (153 kph). Even at this early stage the possibilities of rockets were increasingly apparent, particularly to the military.[20]

Even though Austria was a close neighbour of Germany's, rocket technology did not advance at the same pace. When the Austrian scientist Franz von Hoefft of the Vienna *Gesellschaft für Höhenforschung* (Society for Altitude Research) suggested developing rocket engines in 1928, his ideas were received favourably but the Austrian government lacked the resources to turn his plans into reality. Also, private companies in Austria were less willing to fund rocket research than their German counterparts.[21]

Then in February 1931 the Austrian Friedrich Schmiedl employed rockets using solid fuel to carry mail between the cities of Schöckel and Radegund and Schöckel and Kumberg.[22] This inspired the inventor Gerhard Zucker to attempt to launch a rocket-powered mail service to cross the English Channel. The idea was visionary but all Zucker's rockets exploded when they were launched.[23] Until the *Anschluss*, when Austria was forcibly incorporated into the German Reich, the Austrian government placed little emphasis on rocket development. As a result, none of the early research and testing work was followed up and with a shortage of finance private individuals or firms were rarely able to pursue rocket development adequately.

It was left to the Germans to produce the first rocket-powered snow sled, which was tested on 22 January 1929. This somewhat alarming vehicle was called the RS-1 and it was powered by Sander rockets. It reached a speed of 65 mph (105 kph), gliding along the snow on pontoons. Whether it was built with any practical considerations in mind is a moot point, however.

Nazi rocket takeover

Private rocket development was flourishing in Germany in the early 1930s. Karl Poggensee launched a solid-fuel rocket on 13 March 1931 near Berlin which was equipped with cameras, a speed indicator and an altimeter. The rocket attained a height of 1,500 feet before parachuting to the ground.[24] On the following day, 14 March 1931, Johannes Winkler and his assistant Hugo Huckel launched the first liquid-fuel rocket in Europe, near the city of Dessau. It was 2 ft long by 1 ft wide (0.6 x 0.3 m) and was known as the *Huckel-Winkler 1*. Powered by a mixture of liquid oxygen and liquid methane, it attained a height of 1,000 ft (305 m). Then on 6 October 1932, the *Huckel-Winkler 2* was launched near Pillau in East Prussia, but it only managed an altitude of 10 ft (3.05 m) before catching fire.[25]

German engineer and pilot Reinhold Tiling had more success than most when he launched four solid-fuel rockets at Osnabruck in April 1931. One of them exploded at 500 ft (152 m), two climbed to 1,500—2,000 ft (456–608 m) and one managed to attain a height of 6,600 ft (2,012 m) at a speed of 700 mph (1,127 kph). He later launched two more rockets from Wangerooge in the East Frisian islands. One of them is said to have attained an altitude of 32,000 ft (9,754 m), but no details of these tests survive.[26] His career was unfortunately cut short in 1933 when the powder that powered his rockets exploded and killed him.

The collapse of the VfR through a combination of financial difficulties and the anti-Nazi views of some of its members meant that all rocket development now came under the control of the German military. All private rocket testing ended and only military experiments could now take place.

Von Braun was quite happy to work for the Wehrmacht at Kummersdorf as long as he was working in his chosen field and there he carried out static tests of missiles with an avowedly military purpose. Walter Dornberger, Wernher von Braun and other leading rocket scientists soon designed the A-1 rocket, powered with a mixture of alcohol and liquid oxygen. With a thrust of 660 lb (300 kg) and a 70 lb (32 kg) gyroscope in the nose of the rocket to give it stability, it was hoped that it would be the forerunner of a series of ballistic weapons. However, the design was flawed because the gyroscope had been placed too far from the centre of the rocket and the fuel tank was liable to catch fire. The project was abandoned and its successor, the A-2, was fitted with separate tanks for the alcohol and liquid oxygen and its gyroscope was given a more central location. December 1934 saw two A-2 rockets launched from the island of Borkum in the North Sea, when they attained a height of 6,500 ft (1,981 m).[27] The tests showed considerable promise but the military was not convinced. Hitler was even more doubtful and he rejected a proposal in 1935 to develop a rocket capable of long-range bombardment.

Like von Braun, most of the scientists did not object to working on military projects, however much they may have been drawn to rocketry by the desire to explore outer space. In the course of their work to create long-range missiles they learned a great deal about how rocketry worked in practice and this knowledge later played a key part in the post-war space programme.

Eugen Sänger, an Austrian aerospace engineer, also carried out rocket research under the auspices of the military from 1936 onwards, developing rocket engines burning a combination of diesel and liquid oxygen. They produced a thrust of up to 50 lb (22.7 kg) for half an hour but were rejected as being unlikely to have any military value.[28]

During the Spanish Civil War an original way of using rockets was employed. Rockets normally designed for rescue at sea were converted into craft that dropped propaganda leaflets behind the Republican lines. The nose cones of the rockets were modified so that they burst open and released the leaflets. Militarily this had little value, but it may have contributed to lowering morale among the Spanish government forces.[29]

In April 1937, German rocket development was transferred to a new base at Peenemünde on the Baltic Sea. The rocket scientists began by developing the A-3, a rocket with similarities to the A-1 and A-2, but which was a far superior model. Like its forebears, the A-3 burned a mixture of alcohol and liquid oxygen and by the end of 1937 it had been tested. Its propulsion system worked well, but, as was the case with most of the German rocket programmes, there were problems with the guidance system that controlled the craft. Eventually these were overcome and the scientists at Peenemünde began to plan larger and more powerful rockets.

In 1938, with war becoming increasingly likely, the German military asked the Peenemünde team to design and develop a long-range ballistic weapon which could carry warheads. The specification was for a range of 150–200 miles (241–322 km) and a one-ton warhead. Another stipulation was that the weapon did not have to be too big, for it also needed to be able to travel through railway tunnels and around curves and it had to be possible to haul it into the field of combat on trucks. It was clear that the A-3 was not capable of performing these tasks, so the team at Peenemünde began designing and developing the A-4 rocket.

An intermediate stage between the A-3 and A-4 was curiously numbered the A-5. This had a similar design to the A-3 but with a stronger structure and a more reliable guidance system and its exterior was identical to that of the scheduled A-4 rocket. Between the autumn of 1938 and throughout 1939, tests on the A-5 were conducted. Both vertical and horizontal launches were tried and the rocket was sometimes recovered by parachute. The first A-5 attained a height of 19 ft (5.8 m). It was a small-scale version of what became the V-2.

Some years of working on a variety of rocket projects followed and by 1941 the team at Peenemünde had developed large rocket engines powered by liquid fuel and had solved the problems of supersonic flight. The gyroscopic guidance system and rudders for control and stability were less well advanced but were sufficiently developed to allow the rocket to fly. With more time at their disposal, they would almost certainly have managed to achieve a more successful system of rocket control.[30]

Fortunately for the Americans, Eugen Sänger and Irene Bredt's *Silbervogel* (Silverbird), a spaceplane that was theoretically able to reach any target on Earth in a very short time, did not make it to the starting line. The Sänger-Bredt rocket bomber programme began in 1936 and work on its development continued until 1942. The engine was fuelled with a mixture of liquid oxygen and diesel and it was launched through a rocket-boosting sledge. This thrust the bomber into the air and the booster rockets enabled the plane to reach an altitude of 32,800 ft (10,000 m) within 30 seconds. The rocket motor was then fired after which the plane climbed a further 90 miles (145 km), achieving a flight speed of 13,500 mph (21,726 kph). It was planned as an intercontinental weapon and its designers believed it could hit New York and return to Germany within an hour and three-quarters of its launch. But it was somewhat ahead of its time and problems such as huge heat build-up could not then be solved. After the war this advanced project became the basis of the American *Dynosaur* and the Russian T-44.[31]

Another rocket-powered plane was the *Bachem Ba 349 Natter*, which was a manned vertical take-off surface-to-air missile. Its pilot was supposed to aim 24 RM4 missiles at an enemy bomber and then parachute to safety at the crucial moment. Needless to say, the Nazis were not overly concerned about health and safety and the one test pilot died. The plane was devised by Erich Bachem of Bachem-Werke in Württemberg and construction began in August 1944. It was mainly built from wood and rested on ten 80-ft (24.4 m) long ramps thrusting upwards into the sky. Launched by rocket, it could achieve a height of 35,800 ft (10, 912 m) in a minute.

Three test launches of the *Natter* took place and 36 were constructed. Ten were deployed at Kirchem-unter-Teck in April 1945, but as American forces approached the plane was destroyed. The sole survivor was a prototype in a Thuringian factory which was discovered by the Russians when they captured that part of Germany.[32]

The most successful of the rocket-powered planes was the Messerschmitt Me 163 *Komet*, which was designed by Alexander Lippisch as a rocket-powered fighter plane. This radically experimental aircraft had many problems and only 370 were completed, but its performance was unmatched by any Allied aircraft. In July 1944, test pilot Heini Dittmar flew the plane at 700 mph (1,127 kph), a record which was not broken officially until November 1947. If more urgency had been placed on its development, it might have made a difference in the air war.[33]

The Me 263 was developed from the *Komet* and made its first test flight in February 1945. It was followed by several others that month, but the tests revealed many problems. The most serious difficulty was with the plane's centre of gravity, for which a temporary solution was found using counterweights. It then became clear to the designers that only by repositioning either the engine or the aircraft's landing gear could these defects be corrected.

With the pressure of time and shortage of fuel, test flights were abandoned and the priority of the project was downgraded. Eventually the twin-chambered HWK 109-509C engine was installed, which solved the problem of the plane's centre of gravity, but it remained an aircraft without much support and only flew as a glider.

The aircraft and its blueprints were captured by American forces in April 1945. Some were taken to the United States, some were destroyed and some were handed over to the Soviets. The Russians designed the MIG 1-270 Interceptor on the basis of the Me 263, but as was so often the case the potential for the Nazi secret weapons was rarely fully utilized. A combination of scarcity, the constraints of war and poor judgement by those in charge of military procurement made them less effective than they might have been.[34]

FOOTNOTES

1 Peter Alway, *Rockets of the World*, Saturn Press, 1995

2 Wernher von Braun and Frederick Ordway, *History of Rocketry and Space Travel*, Nelson, 1967

3 Ibid.

4 Sara Madueño Paulet de Vásquez, 'Pedro Paulet: Peruvian Space and Rocket Pioneer', *21st Century Science and Technology Magazine*, Winter 2001–2002

5 Max Valier, *Der Verstoss in den Weltenraum*, Books on Demand, 2005 (original 1924)

6 http://www.firstworldwar.com/atoz/leprieur.htm/

7 Ursula Bloom, *He Lit the Lamp: A Biography of Professor A. M. Low*, Burke, 1958

8 http://www.nationalmuseum.af.mil/Visit/Museum-Exhibits/Fact-Sheets/Display/

Article/198095/kettering-aerial-torpedo-bug/

9 Martin Griffiths, 'Flights of Fancy – Part III: The Birth of the British Interplanetary Society', 30 September 2007, http://www.lablit.com/article/308/

10 Cliff Lethbridge, 'History of Rocketry, Chapter 3 Early Twentieth Century', http://www. nmspacemuseum.org/halloffame/detail.php?id=30/

11 James T. Andrews, *Red Cosmos: K. E. Tsiolkovskii, Grandfather of Soviet Rocketry*, Texas A & M University Press, 2009

12 Michael Stoiko, *Soviet Rocketry: Past, Present and Future*, Holt, Rinehart and Winston, 1970

13 'Giant Rocket Alarms Many', *St. Joseph Gazette*, 18 July 1929

14 https://www.nasa.gov/centers/goddard/about/history/dr_goddard.html/

15 https://www.aiaa.org/SecondaryTwoColumn.aspx?id=1906/

16 Dennis Piskiewicz, *The Nazi Rocketeers: Dreams of Space and Crimes of War*, Stackpole Books, 2006

17 http://www.astronautix.com/r/raketenflugplatz.html/

18 http://www.astronautix.com/m/mirak.html/

19 M. J. Neufeld, *Von Braun: Dreamer of Space, Engineer of War*, Knopf, 2007

20 Rob Arndt, 'Opel Rocket Vehicles 1928–1929', http://strangevehicles.greyfalcon.us/ OPEL%20ROCKET%20VEHICLES.htm/

21 http://www.nmspacemuseum.org/halloffame/detail.php?id=30/

22 F. Schmiedl, *Essays on the History of Rocketry and Astronautics*, NASA Conference Publication 2014, Vol. II, p. 109

23 Mark Wade, 'Zucker Rocket', 28 March 2005 http://www.astronautix.com/z/zuckerrocket. html/

24 http://www.astronautix.com/p/poggensee.html/

25 Von Braun and Ordway, op. cit.

26 Reinhold Tiling, 'Pionier der Raketentechnik', http://technikatlas.de/~ta16/index.html/

27 http://www.aggregat-2.de/geschichte.html/

28 http://www.astronautix.com/s/saenger.html/

29 Herbert A Friedman, 'The Propaganda Rocket', http://www.psywarrior.com/ PropagandaRocket.html/

30 Rowland F. Pocock, *German Guided Missiles of the Second World War*, Arco, 1967

31 http://www.astronautix.com/b/bredt.html/

32 Brett A. Gooden, *Projekt Natter, Last of the Wonder Weapons: The Luftwaffe's Vertical Take-Off Rocket Interceptor*, UK Classic Publications, 2006

33 Jeffrey L. Ethell, *Komet, The Messerschmitt 163*, Ian Allan, 1978

34 David Myhra, *Messerschmitt Me 263: An Illustrated Series on Germany's Experimental Aircraft of World War II (X Planes of the Third Reich)*, Schiffer, 2004

CHAPTER FOUR

ROCKETS AT WAR

Birth of the doodlebug

Speaking at the Langer Market in Danzig on 19 September 1939, Hitler announced that 'the moment might very quickly come for us to use a weapon with which we could not ourselves be attacked'.[1] It is not surprising that British intelligence became concerned and that R. V. Jones, scientific adviser to the Air Ministry, prepared a report. His conclusion was that:

> There are a number of weapons to which general references occur, and of which some must be considered seriously. These include gliding bombs, aerial torpedoes and pilotless aircraft.[2]

As the 'Phoney War' continued (the period between September 1939 and May 1940 when nothing major happened on the

Western Front), it became the consensus view that Hitler was bluffing. Jones took a different view, but his warnings were ignored until the discovery of the Peenemünde site where German guided rockets and missiles were developed, including the V-1 and the V-2.

The V-1 flying bomb was nicknamed the 'doodlebug' or 'buzz bomb' by the British. It was in many ways a hybrid of a rocket missile and an aircraft. Structurally it was a pilotless monoplane made of plywood and sheet steel with a jet engine and with a wing span of 17 ft 6 in (5.33 m).[3] It was guided by a gyroscope which transmitted signals to the rudder and elevator, which acted as stabilizers. A compass was preset to determine its direction and when the required distance had been travelled the elevators were depressed and the pilotless bomb dived towards the ground with its cargo of high explosive. It could reach a top speed of 400 mph (644 kph).

The missile was planned as early as 1930. It was initially known as the A-1 and was designed at Kummersdorf near Berlin by Dornberger and his young assistant von Braun, but it suffered considerable technical problems.[4] Von Braun then

A Fieseler Fi-103 (FZG-76) V-1 rocket in flight, 1944. The V-1 (or Vergeltungswaffe, *'vengeance weapon') was developed at Peenemünde from 1939 on; it was first launched against London on 13 June 1944 after successful Allied landings in Europe.*

developed the A-2, a liquid-propelled rocket with gyroscopic stabilizers, which could fly to a height of 7,000 ft (2,135 m).[5]

In 1933 Hitler's arrival as Chancellor and his anxiety to remilitarize Germany quickly meant that the Kummersdorf site was unsuitable, as it would have presented too easy a target for enemy attack. As a result, in 1935 von Braun recommended that the rocket development and test site should be moved to Peenemünde and by 1937 an experimental facility had been built there. By 1940, the A-4 had been designed and in 1942 it was successfully tested.[6]

When, in 1943, Hitler was shown what these new wonder weapons could do, he reacted with enthusiasm.

'The A-4 is a measure that can decide the war,' he said to those around him.

From that time onwards, rocket production proceeded at full speed. Rockets would be a morale-booster at home and would strike terror into the hearts of the enemy, never mind the destruction that would follow in their wake.

In an unrelated development in 1942, the Argus Motoren company designer Robert Lusser met the deputy head of the Luftwaffe and explained his plans for a pilotless aircraft carrying missiles. Approval was given and work began on the project. Originally this venture was code-named *Kirschkern* – cherry stone.[7]

The first launch of the V-1 proper took place at Peenemünde on Christmas Eve 1942. It was followed by further tests as the first experiments were complete failures. Whenever a cross-wind occurred, the missile was blown off course and the designers could find no obvious reason why this fault occurred so regularly.[8]

The German test pilot Hanna Reitsch volunteered to investigate the problem by flying inside an observation capsule within the missile. She had to lie on the floor of the fuselage and manipulate the controls. This hazardous process continued for several days before she identified the fault. The design was modified because of her discoveries and by May 1943 the V-1 was flying regularly and successfully.[9] Even that was not dangerous enough for her, for she was so attached to the Reich that in 1944 she volunteered to be the suicide pilot of a piloted V-1, signing a declaration which said:

> I hereby ... voluntarily apply to be enrolled in the suicide group as a pilot of a human glider-bomb. I fully understand that employment in this capacity will entail my own death.

In June 1943, reconnaissance planes took photographs of rockets and advanced aircraft at the Peenemünde site and in August the RAF launched a devastating raid on the facility. Nearly 600 RAF bombers took part in the attack and within a few hours Peenemünde was on fire. Most of the scientific laboratories and factories in which work on the V-2 rocket had been taking place were also destroyed.

Panic in London

By November 1943, suspicious sites in France had also been detected. More bombing raids were launched against a range of targets but with limited success in destroying the V-1 bases. The V-1 was launched into combat in June 1944 and caused immediate panic among civilians. Families sat in their homes listening with bated breath to the sound of the V-1's engines. When they fell silent, they knew that it would only be a matter of seconds before the lethal rocket hit its target. A single rocket could claim hundreds of lives and destroy large numbers of buildings. Perhaps even more unsettling was the fact that the V-1s could not easily be shot down.

Londoners were so affected by the V-1's capacity for death and destruction that one and a half million of them left the city, at least briefly. Nine thousand V-1s were launched in total and, if the existence of the Peenemünde factory had not been discovered and most of its capacity destroyed, their effect could have been devastating. As the Allies recaptured France, they overran the bases and the V-1 fell silent at last.[10]

The V-1 was the first cruise missile. It was much faster than most Allied fighters, which made it almost invulnerable, but its weakness lay in the poor quality of its guidance system which meant that the Germans could not use it to achieve the precision bombing of targets. In spite of its capacity for death and mayhem, the V-1's military use was limited by this problem. Civilian lives were lost and property was damaged, but few strategically important sites were hit. It was essentially a weapon of pure terror, designed to intimidate the civilian population and break their will to fight.

Out of these early experimental craft more sophisticated cruise missiles were developed after the war. Their designers overcame the guidance problems that had plagued the Nazis by using advanced telemetry systems and computer-controlled radar, but none of these were available to the Germans. If a better guidance system could have been fitted, the V-1s would have been immeasurably more effective. Once again, the German 'wonder weapons' fell short of making sufficient impact to change the course of the war.

The first ICBM

Just as the V-1 was the first example of a cruise missile, so the V-2 was the first ICBM (intercontinental ballistic missile). It could travel five times faster than the speed of sound and had a range of 225 miles (362 km), but for all its power and distance it lacked an adequate guidance system, like the V-1, so it was incapable

A V-2 missile on the launch pad at Kalbshafen. The V-2 was the first intercontinental ballistic missile. It could travel five times faster than the speed of sound and had a range of 225 miles (362 km).

of precision bombing. In spite of these defects the V-2 not only spread death and destruction but it was the first craft to achieve suborbital spaceflight. After its first successful launch, Dornberger turned to von Braun and said triumphantly:

> This, October 3, 1942, is the first day of a new age of traffic technology; today space travel was born.[11]

Following the raids on Peenemünde a new site called Heidelager at Blizna in Poland was created. Production of the component parts was centralized in an underground factory at Nordhausen in the Harz Mountains. Continuing air raids that inflicted damage even on underground bunkers led to the development of the *Meillerwagen* (mobile wagon) launch system. This meant that the rockets could be moved about and were less vulnerable to assault and it also increased the options for firing positions.

Technical problems dogged the V-2 in its early stages. The rocket often broke up in mid-air and there were 65,000 design modifications before it was ready to go into full production. Once these problems had been overcome development proceeded rapidly, with a thousand rockets being produced between January and May 1944. On 13 June 1944, a test launch was made from Peenemünde. The rocket took off successfully but lost control and crashed into a field in Sweden.

The Allies took full advantage of this failure. The Swedish Air Force collected the debris from the rocket and British aviation experts flew to Sweden to photograph the wreckage and fly the remains of the rocket back to Britain.

Jones examined the debris and compared it with intelligence reports. He quickly discovered that its fuel was liquid oxygen and that it carried a small but powerful warhead.[12]

The V-2 had a sharply pointed nose tapering off from its cylindrical body in which were the warhead, explosive fuses and control panel. The fuses were designed to detonate instantly and achieve the maximum possible blast damage. Its pumps were driven by a steam turbine, with the steam being produced through a hydrogen peroxide and sodium permanganate catalyst, and the tanks were made from an alloy of aluminium and magnesium. Amatol 60/40 was the explosive used, which was detonated by an electrical contact fuse. This was a relatively stable explosive but it could occasionally explode during re-entry. The main guidance system was the LEV-3, with two gyroscopes for stabilization and a PIGA accelerometer for the engine cut-off point. Later models used an improved guidance system of radio signals sent from the ground, designed by Friedrich Kirchstein of the Siemens engineering company.

Silent killers

From September 1944 onwards, over 3,000 V-2s were launched, first against Paris and then London, Antwerp and Liège. Their effect was devastating, both in terms of casualties and the effect on civilian morale. Around 9,000 people were killed by the rockets, which caused widespread panic. At least there had been a few seconds' warning with the V-1, but the V-2s were virtually soundless. A discerning listener might have heard the double-crack explosion of a supersonic device, but that is all. As with the V-1s, if they had been developed earlier and the technical problems had been successfully overcome their effect might have changed the course of the war.[13] The V-2 was infinitely more dangerous, both militarily and in terms of its effect on civilian morale, than the V-1, but each was a weapon with the potential to win the war in spite of the hopeless military situation in terms of conventional warfare.

Project Zossen was first suggested in 1942 by the military authorities in Zossen, a suburb of Berlin. The plan was to 'bundle together' five V-2 rockets and fire them simultaneously, to attain more lift and greater penetrative range. Two designs for this project were produced and wind tunnel testing was undertaken.

Whether these 'bundle rockets' were ever launched in anger is unclear. The only pointer to their possible use is a strange report from the Soviet Union in the 1960s, which gives an account of a German raid that destroyed a Russian munitions factory located in the Ural Mountains, deep in the heart of the country. The Russians described it as a 'terror attack' and compared it with American B-52 bombers and their aerial assault on Vietnam.

By 1945, when the raid was supposed to have taken place, the Germans had almost no heavy bombers capable of mounting such an attack. There were very few that could have made the long journey and with the Soviets enjoying total air superiority over Russia it is hard to see how the German bombers could possibly have got through, still less successfully have bombed a munitions factory well to the east of their capabilities.

If the munitions factory had been destroyed by German action at this exceptionally late date in the war it is more likely that the damage was caused by a bundle rocket rather than by conventional bomber aircraft. The Luftwaffe was incapable of any kind of offensive aerial campaign whereas the rockets, though slowly being eliminated, remained a potent force almost to the end. The idea that the munitions factory was the victim of a bundle rocket attack seems the most probable explanation for the event.[14]

New York rocket threat

Hitler had long been obsessed with seeing 'the downfall of New York in towers of flames', according to Albert Speer. He seemed to think that his mighty enemy could be forced out of the war by a devastating attack on its major city. But that could not be achieved by conventional means so he would need to build a rocket powerful enough to make the long journey from Germany.

The A-9 and A-10 series of rockets were designed to be able to attack the eastern United States. They were potentially the most lethal ICBMs yet devised, but the increasing pressure of the deteriorating military situation made it difficult for their construction to take place and the technical difficulties were far from solved when the war ended. The Germans had considered the idea of rocket attacks against the United States as early as 1937, when the Second World War was still two years away and American involvement in the conflict was anything but probable. In 1938, the idea was raised again and the following year saw detailed planning being undertaken.

Although the A-4 (or V-2) had proved very effective against European targets it would not be able to reach the United States. Various ideas were mooted about how to improve its performance and Dornberger drafted a memorandum to Hitler outlining what he called the *Amerikaraket* (America rocket) in July 1940. The A-9 would be a modified version of the A-4 with a much longer range. The first design work on the rocket began in the same year and was intended to give it greater lift and range. Its engine gave 30 per cent more thrust than its prototype and after extensive wind tunnel testing the original wings were replaced.

In 1941, all work on the project stopped but by 1944 it was back on the agenda. The engineers began by modifying the A-4s through fitting swept-back wings that were intended to extend the rocket's range by 470 miles (756 km). The rocket was then launched from Blizna, but the first attempt failed completely. The second test firing was not much more successful, although it became the first missile to break the sound barrier.

It was then decided to mount the A-9 on a booster rocket, the A-10. The A-10 booster was 66 ft high (20 m) and was designed to reach a speed of 2,700 mph (4,345 kph) and achieve an altitude of 250 miles (400 km). At that point, its fuel would be exhausted and it would fall away from the A-9, which would then be able to reach the target under its own power. Because of the distances involved in sending a missile to attack America the design of the A-10 was further modified. This latest version had a cluster of six A-4 combustion chambers, later modified to a single large chamber. Knowing the difficulties they had already experienced with the automatic guidance systems for their rockets, the engineers decided to make the A-9 a piloted rocket. The idea was that radio beacons on U-boats would guide the pilot towards his target. The Allies were aware of the threat posed by these advanced missiles and at a briefing to journalists on 8 January 1945 Admiral Jonas Ingram, commander of the Eastern Sea Frontier, conducted what his PR team described as 'a historic press conference'. Ingram told the assembled press corps on board his warship in New York harbour:

> Gentlemen, I have reason to assume that the Nazis are getting ready to launch a strategic attack on New York and Washington by robot bombs. I am here to tell you that these attacks are not only possible, but probable as well, and that the East Coast is likely to be buzz-bombed within the next thirty or sixty days. It may be only ten or twelve buzz-bombs, but they may come before we can stop them.

The story was reported in the *New York Times* the following day with the grim headline: 'Robot Bomb Attacks Here Held Possible'.[15]

Both Peenemünde and Ohrdruf appear to have seen actual test launches of the A-9 (code-named 'Thor's Hammer', which was another name for the *Amerikaraket*) as late as April 1945.

Three of these test launches saw the rocket take off into the Atlantic Ocean and the fourth was designed to achieve orbital flight. In spite of the successful testing of these rockets, none were ever used in combat.[16]

Japan rocket

If the A-9 and A-10 rockets were pushing the boundaries of what was possible at that time, the designs that followed – the A-11 and A-12 – were impossible fancies, at least for their time. The costs would have been prohibitive and many of the technical problems were insoluble.

The A-11 and A-12 were truly advanced rocket designs that never got beyond the planning stage. The A-11 was known as the *Japan Rakete* (Japan Rocket) and was intended to be part of a three-stage rocket of which the A-9 and the A-10 constituted the other two stages. It was never tested or produced but after the war ended von Braun showed the blueprints to American officers. The A-11 was intended to be used for gliding or bombing missions, but the problems of achieving sufficient propulsive thrust had not been overcome by the time the war finished.

Even more advanced and experimental was the A-12, which was designed as a fully orbital rocket. The blueprint was for a four-stage craft incorporating the A-9, A-10 and A-11 stages before the final A-12 phase. It was designed to carry a payload as heavy as 10 tonnes (11 tons) in a low earth orbit. The A-12 on its own would have had a total weight of 3,500 tonnes (3,858 tons) when it was fully loaded and fuelled and would have been powered by 50 A-10 engines, fuelled by a mixture of liquid oxygen and alcohol.[17] That would have presented a major problem by itself, according to some observers, because the craft would have collapsed under the weight of its engines.

Fritz X anti-ship missile

There seemed to be no end to the number of missiles that were being developed by the Germans. Nothing appeared to be immune to the onslaught and ships too had to face a different type of threat.

The Fritz X was a highly advanced missile system designed to pierce the armoured cladding on destroyers and battleships. It was the first precision-guided weapon to be used in war and for a brief period it was extremely effective. The missile was guided by a Kehl-Strasbourg radio link which transmitted signals to the tail fin structure and guided the missile towards its target. When it first came into operation on 21 July 1943, after the Allied invasion of Sicily, a number of missiles were launched but none of the targets were hit.

Its first successful mission was on 9 September 1943. On that day, the Italian fleet began sailing from La Spezia in the direction of Tunisia. Following the deposition of Mussolini on 8 September, the new Italian government planned to hand over its navy to the Allies. Naturally, the Nazis had other plans and six Dornier Do 217K-2s, all of them equipped with the Fritz X, were sent out by the Luftwaffe to prevent this from happening. They had orders to destroy the fleet rather than see it fall into enemy hands. The Italian battleship *Roma* was hit and sunk with the loss of over 1,000 lives and another ship was also hit and damaged, but it was able to limp to Tunisia and safety.

On 11 September, it was the turn of the US cruiser *Savannah* to be hit by the Fritz X. She was badly damaged and had to return to America for repairs but was not sunk. Then on 13 September the British cruiser *Garda* was also hit by a Fritz X. It too was badly damaged but was towed to Malta for repairs. In the case of both ships there were a number of fatalities from the missile.

The Fritz X caused damage to other Allied vessels throughout the month of September 1943, but they quickly employed jamming devices to prevent signals getting through to the missiles. This ended its effectiveness as a weapon and it fell out of favour.[18]

Rejected missile projects

So prolific were Germany's aerospace engineers that they seemed to produce an almost constant flow of new and potentially successful missile designs, but for various reasons a number of them never went into action. Others were not used to their full potential. Just a tweak or two or a little more time was all that was needed to turn some of the many rejected projects into formidable weapons, but time and resources were in short supply as the war progressed.

Feuerlilie

The *Feuerlilie* (Fire Lily) was a remotely controlled rocket anti-aircraft missile that was designed in 1940. By 1943 its guidance system had been extensively researched through wind tunnel testing and by July of that year it was ready for the production stage, but there was a shortage of suitable engines. Two models were produced. The first model was the F-25 which was tested in 1943 and 1944, but its performance was unsatisfactory. Then came the F-55, which entered production in 1942 but was not finally test flown until 12 May 1944. This missile was more successful than its predecessor and further tests were undertaken, but these showed a consistently erratic flight path. By the end of 1944 this variant was also abandoned. The *Feuerlilie* suffered from numerous technical problems with its guidance and propulsion systems and in spite of a number of test flights it was never deployed in combat.[19]

Wasserfall

The *Wasserfall* (Waterfall) was a variant of the V-2 rocket that had been designed as an anti-aircraft weapon. It was smaller than the V-2 and so needed a much shorter launch trajectory to reach its target, which was an advantage. The *Wasserfall* used a different fuel mixture from the V-2 with a combination of Visol (vinyl isobutyl ether) and SV-Stoff (nitric acid). It also had a modified engine and combustion chamber and was designed to be launched from concealed rocket bases. But although the *Wasserfall*'s manually controlled radio guidance system was perfectly adequate for daylight operation, night-time deployment required a different approach because of the difficulties of visibility. A new control system called Rheinland was used for this purpose, which involved tracking the target through radar. An analogue computer then guided the *Wasserfall* towards its target, assisted by ground control staff.

Work on the *Wasserfall* began in 1941 and the design was finally agreed in November 1942. Testing began in March 1943 but progress was delayed when Walter Thiel, one of the chief engineers working on the project, was killed during an Allied bombing raid.

It was not until 8 March 1944 that a successful test launch was made and by the end of June a further three test flights of the *Wasserfall* had been completed. In total, 35 test launches of the *Wasserfall* were made, some of which were successful and others failures.

The inconsistency of the missile meant that it received limited priority. Writing some years later, Albert Speer, former minister for munitions, believed that if it had been properly supported the missile could have halted or at least slowed down the Allied bombing offensive. No one knows if he was correct, because the *Wasserfall* was never deployed in combat.[20]

Taifun

The *Taifun* (Typhoon), an unguided anti-aircraft missile, was perhaps an attempt to fill the gap caused by the slow progress of guided missile development. Work on it began on 25 September 1942, when anti-aircraft projects received top priority, and two million examples were to have been produced, with the intention of launching them en masse against the Allied bombers. The missile measured 6 ft 4 in (1.93 m) long and 3.9 in (9.9 cm) in diameter and its development was undertaken by the rocket team at Peenemünde. It was powered by an engine fuelled by Tonka 250, a mixture of xylidine and triethylamine. The missile could reach a speed of 2,237 mph (3,600 kph) and reach an altitude of 39,000 ft (11,887 m), but difficulties with the engine meant that in spite of extensive research, development and testing the *Taifun* was never deployed in combat. After the war, improved variants of it became the basis of the American *Loki* and Russian R-103 missiles.[21]

Rheintochter

The *Rheintochter* (Daughter of the Rhine) was a surface-to-air missile ordered by the Wehrmacht in November 1943. Its name came from the *Rheintöchter* (Rhine Maidens) in Richard Wagner's operatic cycle *Der Ring des Nibelungen*. From August 1943, there were 82 test launches and a variant designed to be air launched was also created. In spite of extensive testing it never entered combat, however, and the *Rheintochter* was cancelled in February 1945.[22]

Rheinbote

On some occasions a missile could be designed and tested and then used in battle shortly afterwards. The *Rheinbote* (Rhine Messenger) was a development of the *Rheintochter*. It was a short-range rocket which was intended to be used as a mobile supplement to field artillery. The *Rheinbote* was designed in 1943 and remains the only missile of its type to be used during the war. Its first tests were conducted in 1943 and although modifications were made the final rocket was almost identical to the original design. With a range of just under 100 miles (161 km), it could attain a speed of 4,200 mph (6,750 kph) and carry an 88 lb (40 kg) warhead to an altitude of 256,000 ft (78,000 m).

The *Rheinbote* was simple to operate, being launched from a rail on a mobile trailer. Once the trailer had been aimed at the target, the gantry was raised and firing commenced. Over 200 *Rheinbote* missiles were built and most were fired against Antwerp from 1944 until the German retreat from Belgium. A few were also fired from Holland. It was essentially a scaled-down and simpler version of the V-2 but it was far less accurate than its larger counterpart. At the end of the war the missile's design plans were captured by the Russians but they do not appear to have used it subsequently in combat.[23]

Schmetterling

The Henschel Hs 117 *Schmetterling* (Butterfly) was a radio-guided missile. It was designed in 1941 by Herbert Wagner and then offered to the Air Ministry, who rejected it on the grounds that anti-aircraft defence systems were not needed.

But by 1943 the military situation had changed dramatically and this time Henschel was asked to develop and produce the weapon. Wagner headed the team and the result was the Hs 117. The missile had an unusual shape with its swept-back wings, tail in the form of a cross and bottle-type nose. By 1944, the project was considered ready to enter the production stage. During May 1944, no fewer than 59 missiles were test flown, but over half of the launches were failures. In spite of this lack of success, the Air Ministry decided to order full-scale production of the missile in December 1944. The plan was to launch the Hs 117 from a gun carriage.

January 1945 saw a prototype developed and the intention was to produce 3,000 missiles a month, but in February 1945 the project was abruptly cancelled. Like many other advanced rocketry projects there was not enough time to correct technical problems so the potentially devastating consequences of these missiles were never realized.[24]

Werfer-Granate 21

The *Werfer-Granate* 21 rocket was employed by the Luftwaffe as an attempt to counter the mass bombing campaign against Germany. Fighter aircraft were finding it hard to penetrate the tight formations of Allied bombers and this missile enabled them to attack from a greater distance. It was the first on-board rocket to enter service with the Luftwaffe. The rocket was not particularly accurate but it did at least force the bombers to manoeuvre into a looser formation, giving fighter aircraft more chance of launching a successful attack. It entered active service in 1943 and was used during the defence of Italy, the campaign in Normandy in 1944 and the 'Battle of the Bulge' – the last German offensive in the Ardennes region.

The *Werfer-Granate* 21 was not only relatively inaccurate but also slow for a missile. This made it vulnerable to attack and reduced the speed of the aircraft from which it was launched. In spite of these defects, though, its large blast area made it capable of inflicting heavy casualties. Had it been more widely used and greater attention paid to correcting its defects, it could have had the potential to be a major military asset.[25]

Ruhrstahl X-4

The *Ruhrstahl X-4* was a project developed by the Luftwaffe after the devastating RAF bombing assault on Germany in 1943. Anti-aircraft weapons were given high priority after that time and in June 1943 design work began on the X-4 at Ruhrstahl.

The missile was planned to have sufficient range to attack aircraft from a great distance, so that it could not be hit by bombers. It was fitted with a BMW rocket engine that was capable of reaching a speed of over 700 mph (1,125 kph) and the warhead was a 45 lb (20 kg) fragmentation bomb with a radius of 25 ft (7.6 m). The guidance system was intended to allow the pilot to manoeuvre the rocket into this range but tests showed that the required degree of accuracy could not be achieved.

The first test launch of the X-4 was on 11 August 1944, but subsequent tests revealed problems and different aircraft and propulsion systems were used to try and overcome these flaws. Production did not begin until 1945, when 1,000 missiles were built. The X-4 never saw active service, however, not least because the aircraft finally chosen as its best launcher failed to progress beyond the design stage. Modified versions of the X-4 were used after the war by the French but were later abandoned by them.[26]

Fliegerfaust

The *Fliegerfaust* (Pilot Fist) was designed in 1944 by Hugo Schneider AG. It was also sometimes called the *Luftfaust* (Air Fist). The *Fliegerfaust* was an unmanned ground-to-air rocket launcher which was portable and multi-barrelled and it was intended for use as an anti-aircraft missile. The first model was the *Fliegerfaust* A, with four barrels firing projectiles that were launched by a small rocket. This was followed by the *Fliegerfaust* B, which had nine barrels, all much longer than the 'A' version. Every second barrel fired four rounds and then the remaining five barrels were fired. A six-barrel prototype was built but never used operationally. The *Fliegerfaust* had too limited a range to be effective and although 10,000 launchers and 400 rockets were ordered fewer than 100 were used in actual combat.[27]

R4 (Orkan)

The R4 rocket was nicknamed *Orkan* (Hurricane) and was an anti-aircraft missile for use by German fighter pilots. It used a large warhead carrying hexogen explosive and its effect when it hit was described as 'shattering'. The R4s were generally fired in four salvoes of six missiles, delivered faster than the speed of sound. These missiles could have been devastating but not enough of them were produced in time and they were mainly used by the Messerschmitt Me 262 fighters, although the Focke-Wulf Fw 190s also used them as a ground attack weapon. As so often in the Third Reich, a pioneering concept such as this was not developed until it was too late to affect the outcome of the war.[28]

KM-2 rocket

The KM-2 rocket was first described in a 1947 article in the *Denver Post*, which referred to it as an 'electromagnetic rocket'. It was alleged to have been tested after the war off the coast of Malaga, under the watchful eye of the Spanish dictator General Franco. The rocket was said to have been constructed in Marbella by German scientists, presumably those who had escaped to Spain at the end of the war.[29] It was cylindrically shaped like most rockets, but its propulsion system – supposedly an electromagnetic one – is interesting. The strong probability is that it made use of the research and experiments of Paul Biefeld and Thomas Townsend Brown, which commenced in the 1920s and in Brown's case continued up to the 1950s. The work of both men would have been readily available to German scientists.

Brown evolved a method of overcoming the force of gravity using a powerful electromagnetic charge. By using an insulating material to keep the positive and negative charges apart, he could exert a unidirectional force, which enabled a craft to slide down the 'gravity gradient'. Brown also developed a way of transferring this charge to an aircraft, by inventing an electromagnetic flame-jet generator using a jet engine with an electric needle to inject negative ions into the jet's exhaust stream. Crucially, it was possible to use steam to fuel the craft. It is highly probable that the KM-2 rocket was a post-war development of wartime research by German scientists and its ability to use a cheap source of power and electromagnetic energy made it revolutionary.[30]

Guidance systems

In addition to the piloted rocket version of the A-9 German scientists are also alleged to have worked on automatic guidance systems. They tried (and on the whole failed) to discover improved ways of guiding the missiles, so attempted an entirely different approach. What they did was to miniaturize as many components as possible, both in the rocket itself and in the bomb load it carried. The thinking was that this would enable the A-9 to deliver a much heavier payload.

One unconventional idea was planting a television camera inside the nose cone of the missile. The camera sent a picture back either to the ground crew or an aircraft, after which the rocket could be accurately guided towards its target. This was yet another 'first' for the Nazis – the world's first 'smart bomb'. By 1945, German scientists had been so successful in miniaturizing technology that their camera was ten times smaller than its Allied equivalents.[31]

Through their research into semi-conductors as early as 1940 German scientists had managed to develop the first transistor and in 1941 it was used by the German military in the form of small radio sets, which were capable of running on batteries as well as mains power.[32]

Over the horizon radar (OTH)

Other cutting-edge technologies researched by Nazi scientists at this time included lasers, fibre optics and (most unconventional of all) 'over the horizon radar' technology.

Over the horizon radar (OTH) can detect targets at considerable distances, far beyond the limits of ordinary radar systems. Once an object is beyond the horizon conventional radar technology can no longer detect it, but OTH radar is designed to overcome this problem. One method is to use a shortwave system that sends a signal which is reflected by the ionosphere. The alternative is to use surface wave systems, which employ low-frequency radio waves. Normally radio waves travel in a straight line but at low frequencies the phenomenon of diffraction will lead them to follow the Earth's curvature. This enables the signals to be transmitted over the horizon and thus vastly increase the range of detection.

The first operational OTH system is generally regarded as being the Veyer system, which was developed by the Soviet Union in 1949. William Thaler of the Naval Research Laboratory then devised an American system called MUSIC (Multiple Storage, Integration and Correlation) in 1955. There is, however, strong evidence that neither the Russians nor the Americans were the first in the field of OTH radar and that the real pioneers were Nazi scientists, on whose work the victorious Allies built after the fall of the Third Reich.

OTH and rocket guidance

In their search for a successful rocket guidance system, German scientists questioned whether over the horizon radar could be used for this purpose as well as for target detection. During their research, they experimented with three different forms of that system, which attempted to use the curvature of the Earth to transmit and receive signals. These were called the *Elefant*

(Elephant), the *See-Elefant* (Sea Elephant) and the *Freya*. The *Elefant* was based on temperature inversions in the ionosphere and the *See-Elefant* was a broadband radar system with a sending antenna between two receivers.

The *Freya* was the most advanced of these systems and was described as 'revolutionary'. Instead of employing a single transmitting antenna and two receiving antennae, the *Freya* used a single antenna which transmitted a pulse. This original pulse signal was, after a short delay, transmitted to the antennae at each side of the central antenna. The *Freya*'s system was the first 'phased array radar', using the Earth's curvature to modify the signals it sent. There were three transmitting antennae and one of them also functioned as a receiver. The use of phased signalling enables the system to 'bend' itself 'over the horizon' and thus provide more accurate guidance for the missiles being launched.

Captured German rocket scientists pose with members of the US 7th Army at Oberammergau, Bavaria on 2 May 1945. Among those pictured are Dieter Huzel (left centre, leather coat and hat), Magnus von Braun, Walter R. Dornberger (holding a cigarette), Herbert Axster, Wernher von Braun (arm in cast), Hans Lindenberg and Bernard Tessmann.

More speculative claims have been made for the possible use of this system as a 'scalar weapon'; that is, a massive electromagnetic pulse bomb. These assertions will be examined in more detail when we consider the case of *Die Glocke* (The Bell). What is remarkable is that the Germans had developed an entirely different type of radar system from the Allies and had mastered broadband operation, phased signalling and 'over the horizon' methods of detection and transmission. All of these developments were later picked up and used by the victorious powers.[33]

Rocket research never received the funding and attention it deserved until the course of the war was already irretrievably lost for the Germans. If they had devoted more time to it at a much earlier stage it is highly possible that they might have achieved overwhelming technical dominance. This could have changed the course of the war in their favour in spite of the numerical superiority of the Allies.

FOOTNOTES

1 https://fcit.usf.edu/holocaust/resource/document/HITLER1.htm/

2 R. V. Jones, *Most Secret War: British Scientific Intelligence 1939–1945*, Hamish Hamilton, 1978

3 Anthony L. Kay, *Buzz Bomb (Monograph Close-Up 4)*, Monogram Publications, 1977

4 Kenneth W. Gatland, *The Illustrated Encyclopaedia of Space Technology*, Salamander, 1989

5 http://www.aggregat-2.de/geschichte.html/

6 https://www.bernd-leitenberger.de/a4.shtml/
  https://www.bernd-leitenberger.de/a4-2.shtml/

7 Steven J. Zaloga, *V-1 Flying Bomb 1942–1952: Hitler's Infamous 'Doodlebug'* (New Vanguard, No 106), Osprey Publishing, 2005

8 Richard Anthony Young, *The Flying Bomb*, Ian Allan, 1978

9 Hanna Reitsch, *Flying Is My Life*, Putnams, 1954

10 Alan J. Levine, *The Strategic Bombing of Germany, 1940–1945*, Praeger, 1992

11 Michael J. Neufeld, *The Rocket and the Reich: Peenemünde and the Coming of the Ballistic Missile Era*, The Free Press, 1995

12 Jones, op. cit.

13 Tracy D. Dungan, *V-2: A Combat History of the First Ballistic Missile*, Westholme Publishing, 2005

14 Farrell, op. cit.

15 'Robot Bomb Attacks Here Held Possible', *New York Times*, 9 January 1945

16 Claus Reuter, *The V2 and the German, Russian and American Rocket Program*, German Canadian Museum, 2000

17 Ibid.

18 Bernard Fitzsimons (ed.), *The Illustrated Encyclopedia of 20th Century Weapons and Warfare*, Phoebus, 1978

19 Manfred Griehl, *Deutsche Flakraketen bis 1945*, Podzun-Pallas, 2002

20 Rowland F. Pocock, *German Guided Missiles of the Second World War*, Arco, 1967

21 John D. Clark, *Ignition: An Informal History of Liquid Rocket Propellants*, Rutgers University Press, 1972

22 John Christopher, *The Race for Hitler's X-Planes*, History Press, 2013

23 Ibid.

24 Roger Ford, *Germany's Secret Weapons of World War II*, Amber Books, 2013

25 http://www.deutscheluftwaffe.de/archiv/Dokumente/ABC/b/Bordwaffen/21 cm Wurfgranate/21 Wurfgranate BR Gereat.html/

26 Bernard Fitzsimons, op. cit.

27 Ibid.

28 Mano Ziegler, *Rocket Fighter*, Bantam Books, 1984

29 Lionel Shapiro, 'Spies Bid for Franco's Weapons', *Denver Post*, 9 November 1947

30 Paul Schatzkin, *Defying Gravity: The Parallel Universe of T. Townsend Brown*, Embassy Books and Laundry, 2009

31 Renato Vesco and David Hatcher-Childress, *Man-Made UFOs 1944–1994*, Adventures Unlimited, 1994

32 Ibid.

33 Ibid.

CHAPTER FIVE

THE MYSTERY OF THE FOO FIGHTERS

Early sightings

As the tide of war turned against Hitler from 1944 onwards, he became desperate to develop revolutionary 'miracle' weapons, believing that these *Wunderwaffen* could still save the day. No idea was considered too bizarre. Under his orders, German scientists worked feverishly on a large number of projects, some of them positively outlandish or hopelessly impractical, and many of these devices would have been totally unfamiliar and inexplicable to an Allied observer. Perhaps it is no coincidence that sightings of the mysterious 'foo fighters' multiplied during this period.

Allied pilots in the latter stages of the war reported seeing strange lights pursuing their aircraft. These were given the

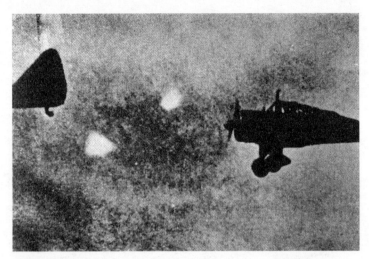

Allied pilots in the latter stages of the war reported seeing strange lights following their aircraft. These were given the nickname 'Kraut balls' or, more commonly, 'foo fighters'.

nickname 'Kraut balls' or, more commonly, 'foo fighters'. There are two origin stories behind the name 'foo fighters', both plausible. One is that a radar operator in the 415th Night Fighter Squadron named the phenomenon after the popular comic strip *Smokey Stover*, the lead character of which had a catchphrase 'where there's foo, there's fire'. An alternative explanation is that it was a corruption of the French word '*feu*', meaning fire. Both may be true and generally the coining of the term is credited to the radar operator.[1]

The accounts of foo fighters in Europe mainly occur from November 1944 and were no longer reported after May 1945. However, the earliest claimed account of a foo fighter sighting took place in September 1941. Two sailors on a troopship crossing the Indian Ocean looked up and saw 'some strange globe glowing with greenish light, about half the size of the full moon, as it appears to us'. They estimated its height as being 4,000—5,000 ft (1,220–1,525 m). It followed them for an hour before it 'just disappeared'. It is difficult to determine what the sailors saw and it is unfortunate that the witness who described seeing the phenomenon waited for some years before telling his story.[2]

Then on 26 February 1942 a report by a sailor on board a ship in the Timor Sea near New Guinea described 'a large illuminated disc approaching at terrific speed 4,000 or 5,000 feet above us'. He said that the object circled the ship and that he then reported it to officers.

They could not identify it as any type of aircraft known to them. The object was kept under observation by the ship for around four hours before it suddenly veered off and disappeared.[3] As with the 1941 report, it is unfortunate that the sailor describing this event did not 'go public' until 1957.

Another sighting was made on 12 August 1942, although the witness admits that he was 'in a highly emotional state; it was my fifth day in combat with the Marines. It was quite easy to mistake anything in the air for Jap planes, which is what I thought these objects were.'

The sighting took place in the Solomon Islands, where he heard 'a mighty roar' and saw 'the formation of silvery objects directly overhead'. He saw no wings or tails, said that the objects 'seemed to wobble slightly' and described their colour as 'like highly polished silver'.[4]

It is difficult to be certain what the marine saw. All three of these sightings are similar but they also contain important differences. The colours of the objects were not identical, nor was their speed or behaviour in the vicinity of the ships. The time lapse between the revelation of these events and their occurrence also makes it difficult to form a clear judgement about what was seen. There were reports, too, of phenomena resembling foo fighters from the Pacific zone of war but the most detailed, recorded, analysed and well-attested testimony to them comes

----

from the European theatre. Numerous contemporary accounts from there are available and have been extensively studied. Some probably represent atmospheric phenomena and others may be misidentifications of planes or other objects, but a hard core of sightings continues to be a baffling mystery.

European sightings in 1942

The accounts of foo fighters in Europe are easier to analyse and evaluate because the sightings are better documented, the descriptions are more consistent and they always appear to take place in a combat context. The earliest report from Europe dates from November 1942. That month a bomber was flying over the Bay of Biscay when the gunner at the rear of the aircraft saw a 'massive' object that had no wings and which suddenly appeared behind the plane. He immediately alerted the air crew, who watched the 'thing' for 15 minutes and even took photographs of it. The object then rose above them and made a sharp 180-degree turn before vanishing.[5]

In the following month, December 1942, an RAF pilot who was cruising over the River Somme saw two orange lights. They climbed steadily and one appeared to be higher than the other. The objects were slow-moving and when the pilot turned his plane they seemed larger and brighter. They then climbed to a height of 7,000 ft (2,134 m) and remained level with the pilot's Hurricane. He made a full turn but saw that the objects continued to follow him, so he dived down to 4,000 ft (1,220 m); but the lights continued to pursue his aircraft. He tried other manoeuvres but the lights tracked him continually. Only when he pushed the speed of his aircraft to 260 mph (418 kph) was he finally able to outdistance them. He said:

> I found it hard to make other members of the squadron believe me when I told my story. But

the following night one of the squadron Flight Commanders in the same area had a similar experience with a green light.[6]

Sightings peak in 1944

The bulk of foo fighter sightings come from 1944. From April until the following year, there were many reports of these strange objects and with the Allied invasion of France in June 1944 a considerable increase in the number of sightings was reported. A ship's crew once saw a dark cigar-shaped object near Omaha Beach, which could only be seen for three minutes before it crossed the horizon. The object had no wings and travelled above the water in a circular pattern. A cigar-shaped foo fighter is untypical of most reports of the phenomenon and whatever it was will probably never be known.[7]

Then in late August of the same year two infantrymen saw a foo fighter during the Battle of Brest. One of the observers described the object as being:

> The same as a railroad boxcar, rectangular not cylindrical. It seemed five times as large as a boxcar. I looked closely for evidence of propellers, wings, or other protruding devices, but saw none of the three edges visible to us. There was absolutely no noise from it. It travelled at no more than 90 miles per hour. We had a long look at it before it vanished over the sea. Neither the Germans nor the American anti-aircraft batteries opened fire.[8]

Another account by a Canadian soldier comes from the following September. He describes a strange encounter 'just outside Antwerp, Belgium'. According to the soldier's account:

At about nine p.m. I stepped out of my vehicle and on looking upward saw a glowing globe travelling from the direction of the front line towards Antwerp. It seemed to be about three or four feet in diameter and looked as though it was clouded glass with a light inside. It gave off a soft white glow. Its altitude seemed to be about 40 ft [12 m], speed about 30 mph [48 kph], and there was no sound of any sort.

I noticed that the object was not simply drifting with the wind but was obviously powered and controlled. Immediately after it had gone out of view it was followed by another which in turn was followed by five others in all.[9]

In October 1944, near Weert in Holland, a group of soldiers saw a 'brilliant point of light' and their officer studied it through his binoculars. He said that 'the object appeared slightly larger and more brilliant – just as a planet would when viewed through field glasses'. It remained in view of the men for around 45 minutes.[10]

There was a different sort of sighting in November 1944, over the Rhine Valley, when two aviators saw 'a huge red light', 1,000 ft (305 m) above them, moving at some 200 mph (322 kph). Two other pilots also saw a 'glowing red object' which ascended vertically, somersaulted and dived. The observers were sure that it was a controlled device and not an atmospheric phenomenon.[11]

Another November sighting was by Canadian army soldiers. They watched as an object that they described as 'like a star' moved eastwards across the night sky from the River Maas in Holland and disappeared after 20 minutes.[12]

Some witnesses reported a single object while others testified to having seen them in groups. November saw the crew of an American fighter squadron north of Strasbourg startled by around ten bright orange lights. The lights moved across the sky at extraordinary speed but could not be detected by either ground or airborne radar. After five minutes the lights vanished.[13]

Another American airman describes how:

> My B-12 crew and I were kept company by a 'foo fighter', a small amber disc, all the way from Klagerfort, Austria to the Adriatic Sea. This occurred on a 'lone wolf' mission at night, as I recall, in December 1944.[14]

A further December sighting was made by a P-47 pilot west of Neustadt, Germany. He observed a gold-coloured ball with a metallic finish that moved through the air slowly. Another pilot in the area saw 'a phosphorescent golden sphere'.[15]

Also in Germany, another strange encounter took place on 22 December when a pilot saw two 'large orange glows' as he flew over Hagenau. They were also observed by the pilot's radar operator. The pilot reported that:

> Upon reaching our altitude, they levelled off and stayed on my tail. After staying with the plane for two minutes, they peeled off and turned away, flying under perfect control, and then went out.[16]

The sightings continued into the following year. January 1945 saw over 60 people observe a glowing object over the sky of Paris. A witness declared that 'it was neither a hallucination nor a temperature inversion'.[17]

Then on 25 March soldiers encamped near Darmstadt in Germany witnessed a group of globes glowing overhead.

Later that evening they watched around seven circular globes, yellow-orange in colour and extremely bright. They described these objects as moving in the same direction but following a specific path. The soldiers were convinced that each object was individually controlled. They descended and entered the forest, after which they were no longer visible.[18]

The speed at which the objects moved varied too. Some moved slowly and others at high speed. In May 1945, a soldier on guard duty at Ohrdorf, 110 miles (180 km) west of Berlin, saw a yellowish-white globe. He described it as being 'brighter than any star, or even the planet Venus'. It 'passed completely from horizon to horizon in about two seconds. Its speed was enormous.' The soldier added that it made no noise and was at an altitude of 2,000 ft (610 m).[19]

These strange phenomena were generally undetectable by radar, but some operators testify to having picked up targets on their radar which, once their presence was known, accelerated and made them impossible to identify or to track further. These became known to radar operators as 'ghosts'.

None of the reports of foo fighters describe landings, crew or any 'hits' by pilots or anti-aircraft weapons on the objects (except for a single instance in the Pacific). The descriptions consistently imply guidance and control which, in the absence of pilots, implies some mechanism for remotely piloting the objects.

Two of the most significant features of the foo fighters were that they were rarely detectable on radar and made no overt attacks on Allied planes. They frequently tracked aircraft and executed aerial manoeuvres either to continue following them or to take evasive action, but they neither fired weapons nor dropped bombs. And in spite of appearing to be under some kind of intelligent control, or at least a guidance system, no sign of occupants was ever detected.

Press reports

In December 1944, the Americans launched an inquiry into the foo fighters. Little of substance was reported, however, their findings tending to 'explain away' the sightings as 'combat fatigue', optical illusions and similar theories. St Elmo's Fire appeared to be the most favoured 'explanation' for what was seen, in spite of the indignant retorts by the experienced pilots that what they saw wasn't anything of the kind.[20]

The first public notification of the foo fighters came in an American press release dated 13 December 1944. It described them as 'a new German weapon'. The term foo fighter soon appeared in the media to refer to stories about the phenomenon.[21]

Time magazine carried a story on 15 January 1945 with the title 'Foo-Fighter'. It reported that what it called 'balls of fire' had tracked night fighters for at least a month. The pilots had nicknamed the balls 'foo fighters'. The story in *Time* described the lights as following the Allied aircraft at high speed. *Time* admitted that various explanations for the phenomenon had been put forward, particularly after-images following bursts of anti-aircraft fire. Others suggested St Elmo's Fire as an explanation.[22]

Another account, heavily censored, appeared on 13 December 1944 in the *Eugene Register Guard*. It reported that 'as the Allied armed group cut new gains on the Western Front today, the Germans were disclosed to have thrown a new "device" into the war – mysterious silvery balls which float in the air'.[23]

A slightly fuller account was published in the 14 December 1944 edition of the *Twin Falls Telegram*. It reported:

> The Germans on the Western Front have produced a 'secret' weapon in keeping with the Christmas season, it was disclosed officially Wednesday.

The new device, apparently an air defense weapon, resembles the huge glass balls which adorn Christmas trees.

They hang in the air sometimes singly, sometimes in clusters. They are colored silver and other shades and are apparently transparent.

No information was available as to what holds them up like stars in the sky, what is in them, or to their purpose.[24]

The 15 December 1944 report in the *Youngstown Vindicator* was more forthcoming. It read:

It could be that these floating silver balls encountered by American airmen in raids over the Reich are another German attempt to create interference for radio communication and detection signals.[25]

A more detailed (and less censored) account of them appeared in the 2 January 1945 issue of the *Lubbock, Texas, Morning Avalanche*. It was written by war correspondent Robert Wilson and the title of his story was: 'Eerie German "foo-fighter" stalks Yanks over Naziland'. Wilson wrote:

The Nazis have thrown something new into the night skies over Germany – the weird, mysterious 'foo fighters', balls of fire which race alongside the wings of American Beaufighters flying intruder missions over the Reich.

The balls of fire appear suddenly and accompany the planes for miles. They appear to be radio-controlled from the ground and manage to keep up with planes flying 300 miles an hour.

> 'There are three kinds of these lights we call "foo-
> fighters",' said Lt. Donald Meiers, of Chicago, Ill.
> 'One is red balls of fire which appear off our wing
> tips and fly along with us, the second is a vertical row
> of three balls of fire which fly in front of us and the
> third is a group of about 15 lights which appear off
> in the distance – like a Christmas tree up in the air –
> and flicker on and off.' [26]

In the December 1945 issue of *American Legion Magazine* an
article appeared with the heading 'The Foo Fighter Mystery'. It
gave a lengthy account of the flying objects that had been seen
by the 415th Night Fighter Squadron, coming to no conclusion
about what they were. It did, however, state that the air crew were
convinced they were some kind of German secret weapon.[27]

One of the most significant facts about the foo fighters is that
once Allied troops captured Germany, east of the River Rhine,
the phenomenon was no longer observed. The area taken by
the Allies had been the site of many German experimental
developments.

Official explanations

From 1942 the RAF had collected reports into what they
called 'night phenomena' and eventually the British and the
Americans shared information. The British were certainly
convinced that they represented a German weapon, although
the official position is that no evidence of anything like the
foo fighters was found by Allied forces at the end of the war.
In a report dated 25 September 1942, the operational research
section of the Air Ministry described 'recent enemy pyrotechnic
activity over Germany'. The report concluded that there were at
least two different types, which they described as 'Phenomenon
1' and 'Phenomenon 2'. Their conclusions were:

These objects are undoubtedly shot up from the ground, either by a rocket with damping to render its trail invisible or by some form of mortar. It is possible that they are projected by heavy flak guns but unlikely owing to the size of the resulting object.

After a lengthy description of the reported phenomena, they concluded:

Phenomenon 1 is probably purely a 'scarecrow' and is not lethal. Phenomenon 2 is probably a flare to assist enemy fighters. 'Flakless flak' if it exists exhibits all the normal characteristics of flak except the brilliance of the flash. None of the above mentioned phenomena are considered to be in any way connected with aerial mines.[28]

British Military Intelligence worked with the Air Ministry and produced its own report in 1944. The data was much the same and the intelligence officers admitted that they were baffled by the strange phenomena. Following the first wave of UFO sightings in 1947, the Robertson Panel (a United States scientific committee), speaking of the foo fighters, suggested that 'if the term "flying saucers" had been popular in 1943–1945, those objects would have been so labeled'. The Robertson Panel identified a key aspect of the phenomena as being the non-threatening nature of their behaviour. St Elmo's Fire and reflections of light from ice crystals were once again suggested as possible explanations. The pilots, air crew and other observers continued to deny these rationalizations indignantly.[29] There is little doubt that the Allied intelligence services knew far more about the phenomenon than they were prepared to allow the public to know and that they felt it was safer to explain them away as 'pilot error' rather than admit that the Germans had devised another dangerous weapon of war.

Combat fatigue was suggested as a possible explanation for the foo fighter sightings at an early stage. In April 1945, the US Navy began to study optical illusions experienced by night fighter and bomber pilots. This became Project X-148-Av-4-3 of the Navy's Bureau of Medicine.

Dr Edgar Vinacke was the lead psychologist on the project and concluded that most of the sightings were the result of what he called 'aviator's vertigo'. Vinacke said:

> Pilots do not have sufficient information about phenomena of disorientation, and, as a corollary, are given considerable disorganized, incomplete and inaccurate information. They have simply adopted a term [foo fighters] to cover a multitude of otherwise inexplicable events.[30]

That soon became the standard explanation of the phenomenon. When confronted with a variety of electrostatic and atmospheric events and with various unfamiliar optical illusions, tired and stressed air crews, particularly when flying at night and in poor visibility, created a pattern out of this chaos of sensations. The result was the myth of the foo fighters.

With growing concern over the effect of the foo fighters on pilot morale, Howard W. Blakeslee, science editor of the Associated Press, gave a talk on the radio. He assured his listeners that the phenomena observed by the aviators, though strange, were perfectly natural. The pilots were simply seeing St Elmo's Fire, the electromagnetic effects in the form of patterns of light which are sometimes produced when an aircraft is in flight. The 'lights' were not 'real', and so radar could not detect their presence.

Several pilots, on hearing this broadcast, protested indignantly against the official explanation for what they had observed. One described that the lights they had seen flickered on and off at regular intervals and were clearly being controlled from the ground. They also described 'an intense sensation of heat', adding that the radar had stopped functioning. Blakeslee may well have been correct in assigning some of the sightings to the effects of St Elmo's Fire, but his attempt to explain all or even most of them away through that effect is an inadequate and simplistic hypothesis that fails to account for the variety of the observed phenomena.[31]

Experimental technology

No one doubts that pilots in combat, particularly night fliers, will be tired and stressed and perhaps ready to identify any unfamiliar phenomenon with a possible enemy weapon. In spite of that, the volume and detail of the reports makes it hard to accept that 'aviator's vertigo' or misperceptions of electrical phenomena can provide a complete explanation. Some of the sightings unquestionably can be accounted for in that way, but there remains a hard core that does not fit in with those theories.

The stubborn 'hard' cases of foo fighters seem to make sense only on the basis of some kind of German secret technology. This assumption is clearly consistent with the sudden disappearance of the phenomenon once the Allies had crossed east of the River Rhine. It is difficult to believe that a purely psychological phenomenon would vanish so abruptly in that way, whereas if it represented secret German technology its sudden disappearance once the research sites had been overrun makes complete sense.

The accounts of foo fighters seem to represent more than one type of phenomenon. Factoring in combat stress, misperceptions of natural phenomena and mistaken identification of flak or enemy aircraft, there remain a significant number of sightings that defy explanation. The analysis carried out during the war by the British and the Americans shows clearly that three or four different types of 'Krautball' were observed by air crews. The behaviour of the foos, while psychologically disturbing, was not threatening, however. Their pursuit of aircraft may have caused stress and panic but they did not behave in an actively hostile way.

Some of the sightings may have been misidentifications of other German secret projects. One possible candidate is fluorescent balloons. These were relatively small and were often released when German planes were near fighter-escorted enemy bombers. Their launch was designed to fool the Allied fighters into breaking contact with the bombers to chase the new 'enemy', giving the German aircraft a chance to attack the bombers.

Another use for these balloons was to lift objects of various sizes and shapes into the air in order to deceive the radar in Allied planes into misreading the landscape over which they flew. There were also Aphrodite balloons, black in colour, which released tinfoil sheets to confuse Allied radar.[32]

Infrared devices

From 1942, British planes were equipped with infrared 'headlights' which allowed them to recognize friendly aircraft and attack only enemy fighters. This invention became known to the Germans, who in turn carried out experiments with what they called 'invisible light'. Albert Speer, put in charge of the German war economy, instructed his scientists to give the highest priority to a DFS (*Deutsche Forschungsanstalt für Segelflug* or German Institute for Sailplane Flight) apparatus using a 'magic eye', a photo-electric device inserted into the centre of a scanning mirror. Originally it was intended to be fitted to the Enzian anti-aircraft rockets (the first to use a radio-controlled guidance system), but as the Allies advanced further towards German positions they captured the rocket along with some fragments of the *Feuerball* and the Mücka detector device. The last item of equipment helped the pilots of night fighter planes detect their comrades through infrared lights attached to their tails and wing tips.[33]

A forerunner of this device was a sensor code-named *Spanner-anlage* (Peeping Tom equipment), that was first developed in 1941 and which detected radiation from the exhausts of enemy planes. It also lit up the target from some distance and tracked the aircraft. Tests by the Luftwaffe were successful but it was considered too bulky a device to be fitted to its night fighters.

Two separate projects evolved out of the *Spanner-anlage* device. One was the Gärtner infrared theodolites used in anti-aircraft rocket stations and the other was the *Feuerball* (Fireball), which was examined in Chapter Two. Later, other projects using infrared television systems were devised to allow distance vision even through the clouds.[34]

Phoo bombs

Another name given to the foo fighters, particularly by the American military establishment, was 'phoo bombs'. This broad name appears to have covered three or four different but related German secret weapons. One of them certainly used klystron tubes that pulsated at the same frequency as Allied radar in order to jam radar systems on aircraft. This method was discovered by the Oberpfaffenhofen Aircraft Radio Research Institute. They also experimented at the same facility with semi-conductor research to generate radio waves through vibrating crystals.

Other weapons described in the same US report as 'phoo bombs' are two gas devices. One was designed to destroy aircraft engines through wrecking the ignition system and the other gas weapon caused the viscosity of the lubricating oil for the engines to break down and thus make the plane's engines seize up.

Another weapon described as a 'phoo bomb' is what the Germans called a *Motorstoppmittel* (method of stopping motors) and the Americans called the 'Magnetic Wave'. It was a form of X-ray device intended to disable radar and aircraft engines and although precise details are sketchy it may also have been based on laser technology.

Friedrich Georg discovered a report in 1945 by the US Strategic Air Forces in Europe with the title *An Evaluation of German Capabilities*. It described 'phoo bombs' as being 'radio-controlled, jet-propelled, still-nosed, short-range, high performance ramming weapons for use against bombing formations'.[35] It seems clear that many different phenomena and projects were being lumped together by the Allies as they were not sure exactly what type of weapons the Germans were using.

Wiener-Neustadt projects

Several experimental projects were carried out on the site of Wiener-Neustadt in Austria. Some were under the direction of Alexander Lippisch while others were in the hands of SS-based scientists and engineers. The destruction of many of the experimental craft and their technical data makes it necessary to rely on the few surviving accounts by contemporaries. They mention many devices, including balls of fire, gas weapons, electromagnetic anomalies and radar jamming systems. There seems little doubt that the 'foo fighters' were a combination of sightings of various German weapons. That is confirmed by the few available reports from British and American intelligence sources and from the testimony of others.

Whether or not we accept the testimony of those who witnessed the foo fighters, the evidence given by a tiny handful of people who were involved with these projects is perhaps harder to refute. An interesting letter from the physicist Friedrich Lachner to Professor Alois Fritsch speaks of an aircraft factory at Wiener-Neustadt where a model was built of a vehicle with a diameter of 5 m (16 ft) that made a test flight to Vienna. His wife then witnessed an elliptically shaped object flying in the dusk, which made several abrupt directional changes. She thought it might have been an enemy plane and was frightened.

Another witness saw a model of the same craft inside the plant but had no idea what it was and an astronomer working at the factory also confirmed that she had seen this vehicle there. These vehicles seem to have been made in ever-increasing sizes, because a further engineer claimed that he had seen a similar craft with a diameter of 15 m (49 ft). Lachner himself claimed to have seen one such vehicle with a 30 m (98 ft) diameter and believed it was part of a project run by the German aeronautical engineer Klein. His account stated that Klein had developed several remote-controlled craft with a similar span, which were used during Allied bombing raids, though Lachner had no idea what their purpose was.[36]

A former flying officer told the New York press, during the early flying saucer wave, that 'it is quite possible that the flying saucers are the latest development of a "psychological" anti-aircraft weapon that the Germans had already used'.

He added that 'during night missions over western Germany I happened to see on several occasions shining discs or balls that "followed" our formations'.[37]

Kugelblitz and Feuerball devices

Renato Vesco has researched the subject of 'foo fighters' more extensively than any other investigator of Nazi secret weapons. He believes that they were either sightings of the Kugelblitz and Feuerball devices or variants of them. His theory is that they represented a guided flak mine controlled remotely from the ground. The klystron tubes within them were intended to disrupt aircraft navigation systems and force the planes to crash.

The biggest drawback with Vesco's explanation is the absence of any reports of planes crashing as a result of encountering foo fighters. Air crew also noted with surprise that although the globes manoeuvred and pursued them they never attacked their planes. One pilot even flew directly at a foo fighter and it dispersed without any apparent harm to the Allied aircraft.

The foo fighters appear to have jammed or at least interfered with Allied radar, but there is no evidence, except for a single example, that they ever successfully 'downed' an enemy aircraft. They seem to have been able to 'interfere' with the operation of aircraft but to have been unable to disable them sufficiently to cause them to crash.

Vesco is probably correct when he identifies the foo fighters as a German secret weapon and suggests that some of the observed phenomena might represent the *Kugelblitz* or *Feuerball* devices. His idea that they might have been a guided flak mine is one that was considered by Allied investigators but dismissed as unlikely. Flak phenomena, 'flakless' or otherwise, may well have played a part in the sightings but they certainly cannot account for the manoeuvrability of the observed objects and flak would certainly have caused some casualties. It is also doubtful whether the *Kugelblitz* and the *Feuerball* were responsible for all of the observed sightings.

It is clear from the available evidence that no single theory can explain the phenomenon of foo fighters. Some sightings were undoubtedly hallucinations brought about by stress. Others were perhaps misperceptions of natural phenomena and in particular ball lightning and some may have been balloons or even German planes.

It is highly probable that a combination of German weapons was responsible for the hard core of sightings and encounters that cannot be explained. The *Kugelblitz*, the *Feuerball* and the various other types of globe described by witnesses probably account for most of the strange objects observed by Allied pilots. The destruction of the devices and their technical specifications means that the truth will never be established with certainty.

Did some foo fighters, or at least blueprints for them, survive the war? We cannot be certain, but the reluctance of successive American governments to release their data about them is at least suspicious. Perhaps the Americans retrieved some of the information and used it in their own secret projects.

The last word should be given to *The American Legion Magazine* for December 1945. It said: 'Meanwhile the foo fighter mystery continues unsolved and your guess as to what they were is as good as mine, for nobody really knows.'[38]

FOOTNOTES

1 Jerome Clark, *The Ufo Book: Encyclopedia of the Extraterrestrial*, Visible Ink, 1998
2 James Hayward, *Myths and Legends of the Second World War*, Isis, 2003
3 Ibid.
4 Ibid.
5 Vesco and Hatcher-Childress, op. cit.
6 Ibid.
7 Ibid.
8 Ibid.
9 Ibid.
10 Ibid.
11 Ibid.
12 Ibid.
13 Ibid.
14 Ibid.
15 Ibid.
16 Ibid.
17 Ibid.
18 Ibid.
19 Ibid.
20 Ibid.

21 The report was carried in the press by the *New York Times*. 'Balls of Fire Stalk U.S. Fighters in Night Assaults Over Germany', (A.P.), *New York Times*, 2 January 1945

22 'Foo-Fighter', *Time*, 15 January 1945

23 'Floating Silver Balls Latest Nazi Weapons', *Eugene Register Guard*, 13 December 1944

24 'Secret Weapon Resembles Yule Decoration', *Twin Falls Telegram*, 14 December 1945

25 C. E. Butterfield, 'Silver Balls in Reich May Block Radio Signals', *Youngstown Vindicator*, 15 December 1944

26 Robert Wilson, 'Eerie German "foo-fighter" stalks Yanks over Naziland', *Lubbock, Texas, Morning Avalanche*, 2 January 1945

27 Jo Chamberlin, 'The Foo Fighter Mystery', *American Legion Magazine*, December 1945

28 Operational Research Section, Air Ministry, 'A Note on Recent Enemy Pyrotechnic Activity Over Germany', 25 September 1942

29 Report of Scientific Advisory Panel on Unidentified Flying Objects convened by Office of Scientific Intelligence, CIA, January 14–18 1953

30 Edgar Vinacke, 'The Concept of Aviator's Vertigo', Report No 7, US Naval School of Aviation Medicine, Project (X-148-Av-4-3), 8 May 1946

31 Gerald Pawle, *The Wheezers and Dodgers: The Inside Story of Clandestine Weapon Development*, Seaforth, 2009

32 Vesco and Hatcher-Childress, op. cit.

33 Ibid.

34 Ibid.

35 Stevens, op. cit.

36 Ibid.

37 Ibid.

38 *American Legion Magazine*, issue cit.

CHAPTER SIX

FLYING DISCS

Flying saucers are the subject of countless UFO legends, but did the Nazis manage to go one better by building their own version of such a craft? There are a number of accounts by people who claim they designed, built or flew flying saucers under the Nazis, but they often conflict which strains their credibility somewhat. However, Avro Canada certainly built a saucer-shaped craft in the 1950s, abandoning the project a few years and ten million dollars later. Did the Nazis have more success and was the technology lost when the Allies advanced into Germany?

Belluzzo project

A variety of projects involving flying discs were researched, developed and constructed by German scientists and engineers. The numbers are disputed but three were completed and possibly test flown and five, perhaps seven, 'flying saucer' projects are attributed to German scientists under the Third Reich.

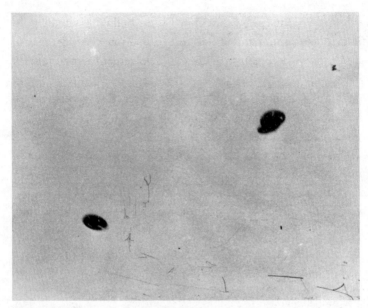

'Flying discs' photographed at Pontiac, Michigan in 1947. Were these aircraft somehow connected to the flying discs researched, developed and constructed by German scientists and engineers during the Third Reich?

The first claim that flying discs were developed under the Nazis appeared in an article by Professor Giuseppe Belluzzo on 24 March 1950 for the newspaper *Il Giornale d'Italia*.[1] Belluzzo claimed that 'types of flying discs were designed and studied in Germany and Italy as early as 1942'. The article included a vague and unconvincing line drawing. Belluzzo claimed that he had developed 'circular aircraft' in Italy as early as 1942 and that his idea had been appropriated by the Germans. He then found himself working directly for the Third Reich along with German scientists.

Belluzzo was a fanatical Fascist and served as a minister under Mussolini. He was an expert on turbine engines and his technical skill would have made him a key player in any attempt to develop 'alternative' propulsion systems. However, in spite of assertions by others that the disc he helped to develop made successful flights and was a piloted craft, Belluzzo stated firmly that it was an unmanned device. He also made no claim that it ever flew successfully. While his involvement in the project is plausible, on the evidence of Belluzzo's own statements the craft was a failure. He did claim, however, that other nations had developed his idea after the war and that by 1950 the disc was capable of delivering an atomic bomb.[2]

His story from *Il Mattino dell'Italia Centrale* was reported in other newspapers and magazines, including *Il Corriere della Sera*, *La Nazione*, *La Gazzetta del Popolo* and *Il Corriere d'Informazione*. The last of these carried Belluzzo's story and a denial by an Italian air force general of the existence of any 'flying disc' programme.[3]

Belluzzo's article was the first to introduce the idea of Nazi flying saucers to the public and it was followed by several others. The Los Angeles newspaper the *Mirror* quoted Belluzzo in 1950 as stating that he worked on developing German flying discs during the war.[4] Belluzzo's flying disc designs were different from the better-known ones attributed to Rudolf Schriever and Klaus Habermohl. His first design is given in the 16 October 1954 edition of the *Tages-Anzeiger für Stadt und Kanton Zürich*, which describes how the discs were designed to take off in the same way as an aircraft. Twelve jet engines powered the disc and the cockpit was set at the rear of the vehicle. A later design attributed to him shows a craft designed for VTOL (vertical take-off and landing). Aeronautical engineers have challenged both designs as being too cumbersome, heavy or badly engineered to be able to fly. Whether or not the designs were aeronautically credible, Belluzzo never claimed that his disc flew successfully. Later, after his death, others made that claim on his behalf.

His failure to claim a successful test flight is a strong argument against these speculative assertions by later writers. Belluzzo was a scientist and someone who was capable of designing a working flying disc. The probability is that rather than becoming an operational aerial vehicle his work never advanced beyond the design and blueprint stage. It does not help that Rudolf Lusar, author of an early work on Nazi UFOs, mistakenly described Belluzzo as Bellonzo. This misidentification led to a raft of conspiracy theories and false trails.[5]

Schriever–Habermohl project

The best-known flying disc project is generally known as the Schriever–Habermohl project. It is one of the best-documented 'flying saucer' stories under the Third Reich. Rudolf Schriever and Klaus Habermohl are said to have overseen the design of the discs. Work on the project began at Prague in 1941 and was originally under the control of the Luftwaffe, but it was later transferred to Albert Speer's Armaments Ministry. Speer then put the engineer Georg Klein in overall charge and in 1944 it was transferred to the control of the SS. The common title for this series of experiments – the Schriever–Habermohl disc – is, however, inaccurate. The truth seems to be that Schriever and Habermohl worked separately on different flying disc projects.

There is disagreement over the degree of involvement the two men had in the design of the discs. Andreas Epp claimed that he devised the original design, but Schriever modified it in ways that harmed its performance. Epp stated that Habermohl's disc followed his design more closely and was therefore more successful.[6]

In December 1965 Schriever was interviewed by *Der Spiegel*, when he claimed to have designed a vehicle powered by a circular plane of rotating turbine blades. The project was overseen by him at the BMW factory in Prague, he said, and continued until April 1945. According to Schriever he then escaped from Czechoslovakia and took his designs back with him to Germany. He continued working on his designs at a workshop in Bremerhaven-Lehe but then both his plans and a model of the device were stolen. Schriever said he believed that Czech agents had stolen them on behalf of 'a foreign power', presumably the Soviet Union.[7]

One problem with Schriever's account is that he told a different story to *Der Spiegel* in October 1952, claiming that his plans were stolen from him on 14 May 1945 at a farm in Rogen, where he was hiding out. One consistent aspect of Schriever's story, though, is that he never claimed his disc flew. An article in *Luftfahrt International* in May–June 1975 entitled 'Deutsche Flugkreisel' (German flying spinning top – the literal meaning is 'roundabout'), created a further layer of confusion. This claimed that Schriever died during the late 1950s, a statement that is obviously incorrect since *Der Spiegel* interviewed him in December 1965. *Luftfahrt International* also declared that on his death papers were discovered, including notes for a flying saucer, designs of the machine and various newspaper clippings about himself and his saucer. The magazine printed what it described as 'reproductions' of the designs, none of which seem technically plausible. It seems safe to regard this article as an exercise in sensational journalism rather than a serious account of a project at the frontiers of aeronautical science.

Epp claimed that his design was the basis for two 'saucer' projects. His original idea was approved by Ernst Udet of the Luftwaffe and handed over by him to Dornberger's team at Peenemünde. Dornberger then tested and approved the design, set up a factory at Prague to build it and ordered Schriever and Habermohl to develop Epp's disc independently of each other. The project was originally controlled by the Luftwaffe, but once Speer became responsible for it he put Klein in charge of the development of the discs. Later still, Hans Kammler and the SS took control. Epp claims that Schriever continued to modify his design up to the moment the Soviets captured Prague while Habermohl returned to his original plan and made three successful test flights.[8]

Another witness, test pilot Otto Lange, is said to have claimed that Epp had designed a flying disc and Dornberger had assisted him and developed it. Those assertions are plausible, but Lange goes on to state that he test-flew the disc for 500 km (311 miles), a claim that is fiercely disputed. In the first place, three men by the name of Otto Lange worked for the Luftwaffe and it is not clear which one is being referred to in this story. More seriously, the German researcher Klaus-Peter Rothkugel compared the letter containing Lange's statement with specimens of Epp's handwriting and found them identical, except for the signature.

More credible is a wartime letter of March 1944 sent from Prague. This describes prototype discs and gives some technical details, but no claims for successful test flights are made in the letter. Three pictures are attached to this letter, one of which shows a disc in flight. However, there is little doubt that these are later additions of dubious provenance and should be treated with suspicion.[9]

Witnesses who saw saucers flying

The Avro Canada VZ-9-AV Avrocar project for a saucer-shaped aircraft was an attempt in the 1950s to create a revolutionary new type of plane. When the venture was launched Georg Klein responded that similar craft had been built under the Nazis and went on to say that two different projects had been developed.

One was designed at Dresden by Richard Miethe, who produced a non-rotating disc which was captured by the Russians during the Allied advance. Unlike his colleagues, Miethe escaped and then went on to work for Avro, according to Klein, on the development of the VZ-9-AV. The other type of disc was developed by Schriever and Habermohl at Prague.

It was a ring of rotating turbo blades around a cockpit. Klein claimed that this vehicle flew on 14 February 1945, achieving a height of 40,700 ft (12,400 m) in three minutes and a speed of 1,400 mph (2,250 kph) in flight.[10]

Another witness claims to have seen a flying disc being test flown in 1943 at Prague. It was 15 to 18 ft in (4.6–5.5 m) diameter and 'aluminium' in colour. The disc was set on four thin legs and it flew at an altitude of 1 m (3.3 ft) for a distance of 300 m (985 ft).

Rudolf Lusar, who was an engineer working in the Patent Office of Germany, gave an account of the Schriever–Habermohl disc. He described it as a cockpit with rotating wing-vanes surrounding it and forming a circle. A band held the vanes in place and the angle of incidence could be increased to provide greater lift. The operational principle resembled that of helicopters.[11]

These discs could be powered by rockets or jet engines. The BMW 003 and the more powerful Junkers Jumo 004 jet engines were researched and considered for propulsion systems while the Walter HWK 109 would have been the rocket engine used for the device. Epp claims that Jumo 211/b engines were also employed while Hermann Klaas stated that the Argus Pulse 307 was considered.[12]

Klein claimed that he saw the Schriever disc fly at Prague on 14 February 1945. A CIA report dated 27 May 1954 quotes an interview with Klein by an unnamed German newspaper (it was the *Welt am Sonntag*) in which he describes his involvement in constructing discs between 1941 and 1945. The CIA report adds that:

> Klein stated that he was present when, in 1945, the first piloted 'flying saucer' took off and reached a speed of 1,300 miles per hour within 3 minutes. The experiments resulted in three designs: one designed

by Miethe was a disc-shaped aircraft, 135 feet in diameter, which did not rotate; another designed by Habermohl and Schriever, consisted of a large rotating ring, in the centre of which was a round, stationary cabin for the crew. When the Soviets occupied Prague, the Germans destroyed every trace of the 'flying saucer' project and nothing more was heard of Habermohl and his assistants.[13]

The claim that the Germans destroyed all traces of the project is contradicted by other sources, which asserted that the Americans and the Russians acquired some of the craft and blueprints and also several of the scientists who worked on the flying discs. Some of the projects would have been destroyed but others survived. Scientists from Nazi Germany worked for both America and Russia and were involved in rocketry, aerospace and interplanetary projects.

It is difficult to know which scientist worked on which projects. The Schriever–Habermohl discs are often referred to as a single project but they seem to have been different attempts by each of the scientists to design the same basic type of craft. Miethe is said to have worked with Belluzzo on the Miethe–Belluzzo disc but even this is disputed. Some claim that Miethe worked alone, while others say that he did so in partnership with Belluzzo or that Belluzzo worked unaided on his disc project.

Trying to unravel these mysteries while hampered by a relative shortage of hard data and eyewitness accounts is not easy, but probably all four men worked on a series of projects. Some may have involved direct collaboration and others lone working while a few may have just required input from the engineers into the projects rather than direct involvement in design and construction.

The extraordinary collection of talent assembled at Peenemünde meant that its team would have been in overall charge of any serious developments. They were involved in rockets, unmanned missiles, engine research, unorthodox aircraft and helicopter design and other flying disc projects were funded and developed under the Third Reich. It is not surprising that some of the claims for testing, and even flights of such craft, are centred in or around the Peenemünde area.

Peenemünde saucer-type device

An account of a saucer-type device from Peenemünde comes from a Russian immigrant known only as Mr X. He told Paul Stonehill of his experiences as a prisoner at KZ (concentration camp) A4 at Trassenhedel near Peenemünde, where he was part of a team of slave labourers working on removing a long-distance cannon from the camp site. September 1943 saw him working at Peenemünde, when he saw an unusual vehicle on a nearby landing strip. It was circular in shape and had a cockpit in the centre. The device, which the witness described as resembling 'an upside-down wash basin', was wheeled out on to the runway on small wheels.

The craft was silver in colour and took off with a hissing noise, hovering at altitude and rocking backwards and forwards. It then jumped into the air sharply and gained height, but a strong wind blew in and it descended to the ground and caught fire. Mr X was aware of a 'smell of ethyl alcohol' and 'blue flames of fire'.

Unfortunately, this is the only account we have of the device and though the use of ethyl alcohol as a fuel for aircraft is unusual, it is possible that with the shortage of suitable substances for aviation engines in 1943 it might have been used. Ethyl alcohol was readily available while more obvious candidates for propulsion were scarce. The story is uncorroborated but it is not unlikely that a disc-shaped craft fuelled by ethyl alcohol was tested at Peenemünde.[14]

Peenemünde is the most likely centre to have overseen any project involving advanced aeronautical engineering. It is probable that the Belluzzo, Miethe, Schriever, Habermohl and Fleissner projects would all have been under the overall supervision of the experts at Peenemünde.

V-7 project

Richard Miethe is one of the few people who claimed that they built a successful flying saucer, which flew over the Baltic on its test flights. Not only that, but Hitler was impressed enough, he says, to order the mass production of the device. If the craft was indeed produced in quantity it seems strange that there is no trace of it.

V-2s at Peenemünde – before relocation to Nordhausen, this was the Nazis'
major base for rocket research and the harbour here could be used for recovering
rocket wreckage from the sea. Peenemünde was captured by the Red Army in
May 1945 and transformed into a Soviet naval base.

In an interview in 1952 with *France-Soir*, Miethe claimed that he worked on a project which he described as the V-7. He said that he produced several different *Flugscheiben* (flying disc) designs for the SS, who were dissatisfied with Schriever's craft and wanted him to improve upon or find a replacement for the *Flugkreisel* (flying top). Miethe also claimed that from April 1943 he oversaw a group of engineers from the 10th Reich Army and that he was involved with research into German secret weapons at Essen, Stettin and Dortmund. Six other engineers took part in the project, he went on, but three of them were dead and the other three were missing, probably captured by the Soviets.[15]

In September 1952 the Italian magazine *Tempo* published some photographs which were alleged to have been taken on 17 April 1944, when Miethe's 'saucer' made a successful test flight. The disc shown in these pictures looks more like a curling stone than any kind of aviation project. *Tempo* goes on to claim that these flying discs were captured by the Russians, who were now concentrating on developing and improving Miethe's design.[16]

In Miethe's interview in *France-Soir*, he stated categorically that:

> If flying saucers exist, it is the V-7 which I built in 1944, the engines of which the Russians seized at Breslau. One of the engines was intended for a supersonic helicopter. The appearance of this apparatus, at a distance of several thousand metres, could, without magnifying glasses, more or less resemble the saucer of a set of tableware. In fact, a helicopter is very different, in its structure as well as its form.
>
> To describe it in common terms, this apparatus has the exact shape of an Olympic discus, an

immense metal disc of circular form, with a diameter of approximately forty-two metres (138 ft). More than twenty months of experiments, continually revised designs and extremely complicated studies of gyroscopy and innumerable tests, which resulted in the death of 18 pilots, were necessary to build these machines.

The problem was that of finding the ideal aerodynamic form that could break the sound barrier and easily transport bombs to ranges of over 20,000 km (12,427 miles), guided by radio and radar, and driven by means of a compressed gas based on helium. 22 cubic metres (777 cu ft) of this gas were enough to maintain an average of sixteen hours of flight. The principle of propulsion was, roughly speaking, that of the jet, but instead of two, or four or eight turbines, the apparatus uses twelve of them, laid out at equal distances inside a moving metal ring, turning around the central mass. There are neither visible flames nor smoke, because the gases coming from combustion are recovered by an extremely clever compression system, discovered in 1938 by a British engineer.

The first conclusive flights were accomplished above the Baltic, three days exactly after the beginning of the offensive by von Rundstedt in the Belgian Ardennes, and with the greatest success. But it was only when Patton's army succeeded in crossing the Rhine that Hitler, warned by Marshal Keitel of the long range of this apparatus, which we had by then named the V-7, decided to undertake mass production in the underground factories of the south of Germany.

Propulsion systems

Some of the various propulsion systems used during these experiments included alcohol rocket engines, hydrogen peroxide turbines, coal-dust ramjets, gelatinous organic/metallic fuelled total reaction turbines and LOX turbine systems. Even more daring was the model designed by Miethe and based on the ideas of the Austrian physicist Karl Nowak. This used a mixture of oxygen and nitrogen.

The power plant effectively burned air as a reciprocating engine was built that used the oxygen in the atmosphere to oxidize nitrogen. High intensity electrical discharges were used to create temperatures of around 50,000 degrees in the combustion chamber, producing the same effects as lightning. The air engine injected exceptionally cold helium into the combustion chamber both to cool the chamber itself and to cause a massive expansion during the heating process, thereby adding to the driving force of the engine.[17]

The idea that Miethe worked on flying disc projects is not implausible. It is, however, impossible to believe that German scientists could have acquired helium during the war. The United States under Roosevelt was consistently hostile to the Third Reich before the outbreak of war and denied the Germans access to helium even in peacetime. This fact alone makes the plausibility of the Nowak helium-cooling system very limited. The Germans tried alternative fuels and apart from helium all are credible for use in propulsion systems. It is not easy to see how the Nazis could have obtained helium even in minute quantities though, let alone the large amounts that would have been needed for a programme on this scale.

More probable sources of propulsion for the craft would have been provided by the engine devised by the French engineer René Leduc. This was acquired by the Germans after they conquered France and there are considerable similarities between his engine and the Miethe–Belluzzo device. Leduc's engine was a radial-flow jet engine which was contained within the metal bodywork of the disc. Although it rotated, no moving parts were visible when viewed from the outside. Air flowed around the rotating engine and between the engine and the metal framework.

There is no definite proof that this device was developed by the Germans but it fits in well with the reported designs of the Miethe–Belluzzo 'saucer'. It was capable of powering a successful flying machine as John Frost proved after the war, when he used it to propel his *Flying Manta* on 7 July 1947 over Phoenix, Arizona.[18]

There is a strong resemblance between Leduc's engine and the first and third of the blueprints offered in support of the Miethe–Belluzzo saucer. It is too much to assert that it was the motive power of the craft but it is the most probable candidate. Research and development of circular-winged aircraft, disc-shaped unmanned vehicles and possibly some type of manned flying disc perhaps took place under the Third Reich. However, it is difficult to be more definite as so much evidence has been destroyed and much surviving data is inconsistent or contradictory.

Flugscheibe (flying disc)

Heinrich Fleissner's 'flying saucer' is perhaps the most credible of all the contenders, if only because he filed a patent application for it in 1955.

Fleissner, who was an expert in fluid mechanics and boundary layer flow, worked at Peenemünde during the war years on what he described as a *Flugscheibe* (flying disc). Fleissner's *Flugscheibe* is sometimes described as a *Dusenscheibe* (nozzle disc) and is said to have flown from Berlin towards the end of April 1945.

There are three wartime photographs of the *Flugscheibe* which show a small saucer-shaped craft with a wing through which air is sucked in via a ring. They also show an external directional control which operated by means of a rudder mounted on top of the cockpit. The 'saucer' would rotate which would then turn the rudder.

One of the pictures depicts two fuel drums on top of the saucer and a third one clearly shows it flying above some buildings.

Confirmation that Fleissner worked on a saucer-type craft comes from an article in a Swedish newspaper in October 1952. This reports that 'a space ship' in the shape of a saucer was designed by Wernher von Braun and his team. A test model flew in April 1944 which was just over 45 yd (41 m) in diameter and could fly at an altitude of over 186 miles (300 km). According to the article, both American and Russian scientists had the technical drawings for the 'space ship'. The newspaper claims that it flew well but made huge demands on the limited German fuel resources.[19]

Further evidence for the genuineness of this 'flying saucer' story comes from Fleissner. On 28 March 1955, he filed a patent application with the US Patent Office for – a flying saucer. The engine for the craft was placed on the outside of the disc and rotated around the cockpit. Propulsion was through starter rockets but the motor was a type of ramjet, where air was sucked in through slots on the surface. The airflow was directed through a rudder and flaps running parallel to the main cabin and a combination of a gyroscope, servo-motor and electromagnets controlled the rotation of the cockpit, either turning it or holding it stationary.

In his patent, Fleissner stated that the craft was capable of being powered by a range of different fuels, including 'liquid, dust, powder, gas or solid'. It could even have acted as a rocket.

The varieties of possible fuels mean that it could run as a ramjet on ordinary jet fuel but it could also, with liquid hydrogen and oxygen, have been capable of flying outside the atmosphere.

Fleissner's patent shows the influence of Prandtl and Lippisch on his design, because the slots at the perimeter of the saucer sucked in the boundary layer while the jets below blew it off the surface. The saucer was effectively a single circular wing which rotated and thereby it could not only attain supersonic speed but it could virtually eliminate drag. Fleissner's design was a true circular aircraft which virtually overcame boundary layer problems. It may have made only a brief test flight but it represents yet another 'first' for Nazi scientists.[20]

Of all the various 'saucer' projects Fleissner's is the best-documented and most supported by the available evidence – wartime photographs, the Swedish newspaper article in 1952, his patent application in 1955 and a magazine article in 1980 where more details of his activities relating to disc-shaped craft are given.[21] Fleissner was a skilled and experienced aeronautical engineer and with the resources made available to him by the Third Reich it is possible that he might have developed a successful flying disc for the regime.

Did any flights take place?

There are two claimed flights for the Habermohl version of the Schriever–Habermohl design. Habermohl himself is an elusive character, though, and some researchers in the field question whether he ever existed. Belluzzo and Schriever certainly did, but neither of them claimed that their disc projects flew successfully.

Klein was the first person to claim that the discs had flown. There are other witnesses besides him, but he was the originator of that claim. We have seen evidence of successful test flights of Fleissner's *Flugscheibe* and a claim that it flew successfully in late April 1945.

It has also been claimed that models of the Miethe–Belluzzo 'saucer' were test flown from 1943 onwards. One of these flights allegedly took off from Stettin but crashed in Spitsbergen. Norbert Jürgen-Ratthofer and Ralf Ettl, a pair of UFO 'researchers', claim that a manned test flight of the device took place in December 1944[22] but both are highly dubious as 'sources' and as neither Miethe nor Belluzzo claimed that their craft flew successfully it seems safe to dismiss their unsupported assertion.

Although Miethe did not claim that the Miethe–Belluzzo craft flew, in a *France-Soir* interview in 1952 he maintained that he worked on a separate 'flying saucer' project in 1944, the V-7, and that it flew 'with the greatest success'. Whether the device was a flying saucer and whether it flew or even existed is the subject of some speculation, however.

So how feasible is it that any flights took place? There are various designs of several different craft and some appear aerodynamically implausible while others are more credible. The range of designs offered is surprising with Lusar suggesting that the Schriever–Habermohl disc was essentially a helicopter that flew at supersonic speeds. One or two photographs are offered in evidence and claim to depict the craft in flight. If the successful flight took place in February 1945 the picture allegedly showing its flight cannot be genuine since it clearly depicts a summer landscape. The 1943 flight has only the testimony of a single eyewitness some years after the alleged events.

Photographs of the Fleissner *Flugscheibe* appear the most likely to be genuine and not only date from during the war but show a plausible-looking craft in flight. Given that Fleissner was a member of the Peenemünde team his device is perhaps the most likely of all the candidates for a Nazi flying saucer. It represents a genuine flying disc project that managed to achieve at least a successful test flight. This is the best-documented and most feasible of all the claims for successful flights of disc-shaped aircraft. Many more attempts were made but the Fleissner project was the most successful of these projects.

A conveniently anonymous source claims to have worked with the Horten brothers. His account declares that he was working at an airbase in Prague and that on several occasions he 'heard' a 'disc-shaped vehicle' being test flown. According to him, it was absolutely forbidden for anyone in the vicinity of the base to look out of the windows on pain of death and all the windows in nearby homes were blacked out to prevent them from witnessing these secret projects. The anonymous 'source' also claims that the noise made by the craft was 'deafening'. There were allegedly five engines which he described as being 'not jet engines' but kerosene-fuelled turbines that could attain extremely high speeds. The 'source' produced a drawing which he claimed was of the Schriever disc. It used rotating metallic vanes to achieve a similar kind of lift to that of a helicopter. He claims that the first test flight took place as early as 1942.

After the war, the 'source' declares, the Americans and the Russians split the 'spoils' of Nazi research between them and began work on developing their own variants on the disc-shaped flying vehicles. That statement is probably the only 'fact' in an otherwise speculative and unsupported series of improbable claims because the CIA considered the possibility that UFOs were based on the Horten brothers' technology during the height of the Cold War.[23]

All of these craft are described as having operated at or beyond the sound barrier and in most cases as having been test flown with pilots. However, both the supersonic nature of these flights and the various designs of the craft have been disputed. The aerospace writer Hans Justus Meier believes that if the discs had the large frontal areas that are generally attributed to them it would have been impossible for them to have flown at supersonic speeds. With the power plants available, aerodynamic resistance would have slowed down the craft and prevented them from breaking the sound barrier.[24]

Some Nazi aircraft did manage to break the sound barrier; Project 8-346 for instance, which was a research aircraft with swept-back wings that was specifically designed to fly at supersonic speeds. It was intended to fit the plane with two Walter HWK 109 rocket engines, one of the propulsion systems that were considered for the Schriever–Habermohl disc. It is known that the Messerschmitt Me 262 also broke the sound barrier in 1945, when the pilot made an emergency dive to assist another German aviator in difficulties. He felt the aircraft shake and experienced unpleasant vibrations as he did so. We have seen in an earlier chapter that there is clear evidence that German aircraft successfully broke the sound barrier during the war on more than one occasion.

Whether any of the flying disc designs succeeded in breaking the sound barrier remains open to conjecture, but if they flew successfully they could have achieved supersonic flight.

The notion that the Nazis were able to develop a successful nuclear bomb is almost incredible yet there is sufficient evidence to suggest that it is true. There is no doubt that research projects related to fitting nuclear warheads to rockets and atomic engines to aircraft took place and that prototypes were designed and built. The idea of swept wing and circular aircraft undoubtedly attracted funding, research and development.

It is possible that these disparate lines of research were combined in a blueprint for a nuclear-powered 'flying saucer', but it is clear that any such research did not lead to it being successfully developed during the war.

In the following chapter the Nazi nuclear programme will be examined in detail.

FOOTNOTES

1 Giuseppe Belluzzo, 'Il Dischi Volanti furono ideati nel 1942 in Italia in Germania', *Il Giornale d'Italia*, 24–25 March 1950

2 *Il Mattino dell'Italia Centrale*, 27 March 1950

3 *Il Corriere d'Informazione*, 29–30 March 1950

4 'Flying Discs "Old Story", Says Italian', *Mirror*, 24 March 1950

5 Rudolf Lusar, *German Secret Weapons of the Second World War*, Neville Spearman, 1960

6 Andreas Epp, *Die Realität der Flugscheiben*, Michaels, 2002

7 *Der Spiegel*, December 1965

8 Epp, op. cit.

9 Henry Stevens, *Hitler's Flying Saucers*, Adventures Unlimited, 2012

10 Werner Keller (interview with Georg Klein), 'Erste Flugscheibe Flog 1945 in Pragenthüllt Speers Beuaftrager',*Welt Am Sonntag*, 26 April 1953

11 Lusar, op. cit.

12 Stevens, op. cit.

13 Report quoted in Stevens, op. cit.

14 This account was first published in *UFO Magazine*, volume 10, number 2 in 1995 and was related by the Russian immigrant Paul Stonehill. His story is given in Stevens, op. cit.

15 Richard Miethe, 'German Engineer Richard Miethe Affirms to *France-Soir*: "If flying saucers exist, it is the V7 which I built in 1944, the engines of which the Russians seized at Breslau"', *France-Soir*, 7 June 1952

16 'La Russia ha la chiave del prodigisio secreto', *Tempo*, 6 September 1952

17 Miethe, *France-Soir*

18 http://aerostories.free.fr/constructeurs/leduc/page7.html/

19 Article in *Aftonbladet*, 10 October 1952; cited in Stevens, op. cit.

20 Heinrich Fleissner, 'Rotating Jet Aircraft with Lifting Disc Wing and Centrifuging Tanks', US Patent Number 2,939,648, granted 7 June 1960

21 Reinhardt Sandner, 'Der Vater der fliegenden Untertasse ist ein alter Ausburger', *NeuePresse*, Number 19/17, 1980

22 Their claim is made in a video, 'UFOs Das Dritte Reich Slägt zurück', Tempelhof Gesellschaft, 1988

23 Michael D. Swords, 'UFOs, the Military, and the Early Cold War', in: David M. Jacobs, *UFOs and Abductions: Challenging the Borders of Knowledge*, University Press of Kansas, 2000

24 Hans Justus Meier, *Die Miethe-Flugscheibe eine reichlich nebulöse Erfindung*, Flieger-Kalendar 1995, E. S. Mettler, 1995

CHAPTER SEVEN

THE NAZI NUCLEAR PROGRAMME

The Germans were among the leading pioneers in nuclear research from the beginning of the 20th century. Many of the experts in the field were Jewish, who fell out of favour when the Nazis took power and left the country. Their previous research, of course, remained available to German scientists and many of the exiles produced scientific papers in Britain and America that the Germans scanned eagerly for possible improvements to their nuclear researches.

Nazi scientists devoted considerable time and resources to developing a nuclear programme. Unlike the American project, this was focused on non-military uses for nuclear energy rather than just creating a bomb. From the beginning of the Nazi era the potential of the atom as a source of fuel was actively pursued. German scientists called atomic reactors 'uranium machines' and the prospect of generating electricity and powering aeroplanes and submarines was researched.

The German atomic programme has often been dismissed or written off as a failure. It was said to be based on incorrect principles and wrong approaches and many of the scientists working on the project were accused of lacking enthusiasm for the development of atomic research. That comfortable viewpoint can no longer be sustained and the significant progress of Nazi scientists in atomic physics is another factor that may have weighed on Patton's mind when he made his pessimistic diary entry about losing the war.

Heinz Ewald, later a member of the Uranium Club, proposed an electromagnetic isotope separator. This idea found favour with the wealthy Manfred von Ardenne, who had set up his private research laboratory facilities in Berlin. Originally von Ardenne was interested in researching the fields of electron microscopy, radio and television. He produced several inventions and his important contacts allowed him to continue his research.

Von Ardenne's *Forschungslaboratoriums für Elektronenphysik* (Laboratories for the Physics of Electrons) then became involved in research into nuclear physics. He obtained finance for these projects from the RPM (*Reichspostministerium* – Reich Postal Ministry).

Von Ardenne recruited senior scientific figures to work in his laboratories, the most prominent being the nuclear physicist Fritz Houtermans, but he also conducted his own research into the separation of isotopes as well as employing other scientists. Following Ewald's advice, he began to build a prototype machine, but shortages of material and staff and the increasing difficulties of the war meant that his project was never successfully completed.[1] Von Ardenne later surrendered to the Russian forces and became part of the Soviet nuclear weapons project.

Nuclear fission

In December 1938, the German chemist Otto Hahn and his assistant Fritz Strassmann wrote to *Naturwissenschaften* (Natural Sciences), a scientific journal. Their article was published in the 6 January 1939 issue of the magazine and described how they had identified barium following the process of bombarding uranium with neutrons.[2]

Before publication Hahn sent his results to the Jewish scientist Lise Meitner, his friend and colleague, who had gone into exile in Sweden. She checked and confirmed Hahn's results and her nephew Otto Frisch gave the process the name 'nuclear fission'. Frisch also confirmed Hahn's results experimentally on 13 January 1939.[3] Scientists had been attempting to use the atom to generate energy for many years and Hahn's success excited the physics community. The age of atomic power was about to begin and it is ironic that the process of nuclear fission was discovered by three anti-Nazi scientists, two of them Jewish.

The Uranium Club was a group of scientists who began meeting together in April 1939 to discuss the development and production of nuclear weapons. The group was founded by Paul Harteck and Georg Joos, who both saw the military uses of nuclear power and approached the military with their proposals. They were soon joined by other scientists, particularly Eric Schumann and Kurt Diebner. Diebner was a fanatical Nazi and he soon tried to take control of research into nuclear fission.

Work on the project began at the Georg-August University of Göttingen, but it did not last long as many of the scientists were called up for military training. On 1 September 1939, the Wehrmacht took over the programme and began to direct the Uranium Club into the military development of nuclear power. By late September 1939 many more scientists had joined, including the pre-eminent German physicist, Werner Heisenberg. Diebner remained the driving force in the project but Heisenberg's expertise soon made him one of the most important members of the 'club'.

The scientists focused on three main areas – developing a nuclear reactor, separating uranium isotopes and producing uranium and heavy water. Originally, they worked on the new process of nuclear fission but in January 1942 the HWA (*Heereswaffenamt*) department of the Wehrmacht decided it was not sufficiently advanced to be able to assist the war effort. As a result, they turned it over to the *Reichsforschungsrat* (RFR; Reich Research Council), which divided its research between nine scientific institutes. There was a growing tendency among both the military and the government to downgrade the importance of nuclear fission because of the increasing need for urgent results.

Nuclear power as an energy source

At the height of the military involvement in nuclear physics in 1942 there were 70 scientists working on various aspects of the programme. However, the realization that nuclear weapons could not be produced rapidly enough to be an effective method of breaking the resistance of the Allies led to the military losing interest. From that point onwards nuclear physics was given lower priority and some of the scientists were put to work on weapons with a more immediate impact on the course of the war. The nuclear programme retained its *kriegswichtig* (important to the war effort) classification though, and funding and research and development work continued. It was, however, removed from the HWA and transferred to a series of institutes, each working on different aspects of research into nuclear physics.[4]

German theoretical physicist Werner Heisenberg was a pioneer of quantum mechanics best known for the Heisenberg Uncertainty Principle, published in 1927. Although attacked by Nazis as a 'White Jew' because he insisted on teaching about the achievements of Jewish scientists, he became a principal scientist in the Nazi nuclear weapons project.

Albert Speer then convened a conference on 4 June 1942 at which he instructed the scientists to concentrate their efforts on making atomic power a viable energy source for Germany rather than on the development of nuclear weapons.[5] A few days later, on 9 June 1942, a decree by Hitler reorganized the RFR and removed it from the control of the ineffective Bernard Rust.[6]

It was transferred to the control of Hermann Goering, but his appointment as chief of the project made little difference to its progress. The failure to make scientific headway in the field had not been helped by the attitude of Hitler, who had shown his dislike for nuclear physics by declaring that it was 'Jewish science' and 'a field tainted by Jews'. He was also, according to Albert Speer, 'filled with a fundamental distrust of all innovations which, as in the case of jet aircraft or atom bombs, went beyond the technical experience of the First World War generation'.

'Jewish science' or not, at a meeting held on 6 July 1942 the Nazi leadership admitted that the absence of Jewish scientists – either by expulsion or through their voluntary exile – was a mistake which had led to serious consequences for German science. Not only was their knowledge and expertise denied to the Reich, but many of them now served the country's enemies.[7]

Abraham Esau was appointed on 8 December 1942 by Goering as his representative on the nuclear project and was replaced in December 1943 by Walter Gerlach, but in spite of their undoubted abilities in the field neither of them made significant progress.[8] The results of their scientific research were published in the magazine *Kernphysikalische Forschungsberichte* (Research Reports in Nuclear Physics), a purely internal publication of the Uranium Club in which all of the reports were classified as 'top secret'. The reports were seen by only a handful of people and it was strictly forbidden to keep copies of them. At the end of the war these documents were taken by the Allies and sent to the US Atomic Energy Commission to be evaluated. They were declassified in 1971 and returned to West Germany. Copies are held at the Karlsruhe Nuclear Research Centre and the American Institute of Physics.

Diebner, Esau, Gerlach and Schumann remained the leading lights in the German project to develop the military application of nuclear power and less influential but still involved actively were Heisenberg, Walther Bothe, Carl Friedrich von Weizsäcker, Friedrich Bopp, Klara Döpel, Robert Döpel, Siegfried Flügge, Otto Hahn, Paul Harteck, Walter Herrmann, Karl-Heinz Höcker, Fritz Houtermans, Horst Korsching, Georg Joos, Heinz Pose, Carl Ramsauer, Fritz Strassmann, Karl Wirtz and Karl Zimmer. These were impressive talents but when compared with the list of German émigré scientists they were not enough to compensate for the voluntary exiles. The effect of the loss of Einstein, Born, Stern, Teller, Meitner and Schrödinger is impossible to quantify but it irreparably harmed both the future of the German nuclear programme and German science generally. Many of the exiles went on to work for Britain or America and the results of their work impacted decisively on the course of the war.

In 1933 Max Planck was so concerned about the effects of the regime's anti-Semitism that he met Hitler to try to persuade him to change his mind or at least moderate his policies. He told him he feared the loss of German scientists to foreign countries and that their departure would harm German science. Hitler responded by retorting:

> If the dismissal of Jewish scientists means the annihilation of contemporary German science, then we will do without science for a few years!

After that Planck had no option but to abandon his attempts to save Jewish scientists. He worked hard to allow the teaching of Einstein's theories in Germany and tried to counteract the dogmatism of National Socialist ideas, but with only limited success.

Heavy water

Scientists at Vemork in Norway, engaged in producing ammonia, were the first to notice the curious phenomenon of 'heavy water', which they had discovered as a by-product of their production process. In ordinary water the hydrogen atoms consist of one proton and one electron whereas the hydrogen atoms in heavy water have an added neutron, the isotope deuterium.

Independently, German scientists in the 1930s discovered that some rare isotopes of uranium become unstable and split on absorption of an additional neutron – in other words, become fissile – which made a chain reaction possible, in which fissions triggered other fissions in a continuing process. But all of this would work better, they thought, if something could be found that would slow the loose neutrons down, because slow-moving neutrons are more efficient at splitting uranium atoms. That substance was heavy water, which would act as a neutron moderator. The Norwegian heavy water was quickly shipped back to Germany to be used in nuclear experiments, following their conquest of the country.

The level of 'export' roused the suspicions of the Norwegian resistance and although they had no idea why the water was being taken to Germany, they reported the activities to British intelligence. By 1942, the British were convinced that the Nazis were using the heavy water to try to develop an atomic bomb. A night-time bombing raid to destroy the facility at Vemork was considered but was rejected as too risky. Instead a campaign of covert sabotage was planned.

Allied saboteurs

On 19 November 1942 two Halifax bombers flew through dense winter clouds, towing gliders behind them. Each glider contained troops trained in sabotage, from the 1st British Airborne Division. As they approached the landing site on Lake Møsvatn, in the hills below, still shrouded in winter snow, Norwegian resistance fighters waited for their arrival. The mission was to destroy or at least severely damage the Vemork plant. As the aircraft approached their target, disaster struck. One of the Halifax bomber pilots, confused by the poor visibility, crashed his plane directly into a mountain. The glider pilot managed to escape but was unable to contact the resistance fighters on the ground. The other glider made it through but the noise of the explosion had alerted the Germans, who sent troops to investigate. The resistance fighters knew the plane had crashed too far away from them, so they were forced to retreat to the mountains and wait, but the glider crews were captured by the Germans and executed.

Three months passed before another mission was possible. On 19 February 1943, six Norwegian fighters were parachuted in to join the original resistance group. The ten men set out with rifles, explosives, sub-machine guns and cyanide pills and by 28 February they were ready to attack. Their target sat on top of a 600 ft (183 m) cliff, which could only be reached via a 240 ft (73 m) long bridge across a deep ravine. To add to their difficulties, the area was extensively mined and the bridge was guarded and well-lit. A frontal assault was out of the question, so the Norwegian fighters climbed down the cliff face and into the ravine below. With difficulty, they scaled the cliff until they stood on the other side.

Five of the team acted as a rearguard to protect the saboteurs from German attacks and the rest of the fighters divided into two groups, each armed with explosives. They cautiously approached a basement door that intelligence sources had reported as being unlocked, but the agent on the ground who was supposed to unlock it had fallen ill and could not be there to assist them. This setback did not deter them and both teams separated to find alternative points of entry. Two of the men discovered a hatch which, though small, led on to a narrow shaft containing pipes and wires. A careful investigation revealed that it was possible for them to make their way through the narrow aperture. They crawled slowly through the shaft, pushing their explosives in front of them and hearing the hum of the factory's machines nearby.

When they finally reached the end of the tunnel, the two men climbed down a ladder. They gazed at the target in front of them, seeing a row of metal cylinders lining the walls. Inside the room beyond was the heavy water facility. The two fighters sprang into the room and took the security guard by surprise. He quickly raised his hands as they pointed their guns at him. Locking the entry doors, the men made their way to the heavy water tanks and began placing their explosive charges.

While the team were planting their fuses they were interrupted by the sound of breaking glass from the other side of the room. They drew their weapons, but instead of German troops they saw the other team entering. Both teams now worked together on setting the charges. Another Norwegian worker entered and immediately put up his hands as the armed men pointed their weapons at him.

Lighting the fuses, the team ordered their prisoners to run upstairs before the charges went off. They dropped a British machine gun on the floor to try and mislead the Germans into thinking it was the work of British agents rather than the Norwegian resistance. Having set the charges, the teams made their escape and waited for the sound of explosions. They only heard a surprisingly quiet thud, but it had been effective. The demolition team had not been able to destroy the plant but they had crippled it severely and they were able to retreat to the safety of the mountains before the Germans realized what had happened.

It took the Germans five months before they were fully able to repair the damage. The production of heavy water then began once more, but the Allies struck again. In November 1943, an air attack was launched on the facility by 143 B-17 bombers. They pounded it with over 700 bombs and many missed their target, but the effect of the raid was to make the Germans decide to abandon the plant altogether.

The heavy water within the facility was loaded into a railway carriage and placed on a boat. It was planned to ferry it across Lake Tinnsjå and on to Germany to be used in the German factories. The boat reached the deepest part of the lake when a loud explosion was heard and it sank below the water, taking with it the building blocks of the German nuclear programme. Fourteen people were killed by the bomb, which had been planted by the Norwegian resistance.

The end of the Norwegian heavy water facility did not stop the Nazi nuclear programme, but it slowed it down to a significant extent and it may have been a decisive factor in preventing the Germans from developing the atomic bomb at an earlier time. The actions of the resistance fighters have been filmed and are the subject of more than one book.[9]

Uranium manufacture

Uranium is an essential component of nuclear fission and that is why German scientists Nikolaus Riehl and Günter Wirths were in charge of a project to extract high-quality uranium oxide at the Auergesellschaft factory in Oranienburg. They produced the sheets and cubes of uranium for the various tests they conducted on behalf of the HWA. The plant produced thorium as well as uranium and continued its work until the very end of the war, when it was deliberately bombed by the Western Allies on 15 March 1945. This bombing operation was not directed against the Germans but was designed to prevent its equipment and research from being taken over by the advancing Soviet forces.

Not all of the facilities at the factory were destroyed but most of it was inoperable. At a time when the Russians were supposedly allies, this was one of the earliest 'shots' in the forthcoming Cold War. At the end of the war Riehl and other German scientists were taken back to Russia to work on the Soviet nuclear programme.[10]

Some of the early research into nuclear developments had been extremely promising. For instance, in April 1942 Werner Heisenberg and Robert Döpel were able to demonstrate a significant increase in neutrons during their experiments. The Allied scientists working on nuclear fission did not achieve the same result until July of that year, so at that point the Germans were leading the Americans in the race for atomic power.[11]

However, the destruction of Döpel's machine by a chemical explosion at Leipzig put an end to the early successes because the failure of the Leipzig reactor meant that progress towards developing a nuclear reactor slowed down dramatically. With the increasing priority given to scientific projects with immediate military application, the German nuclear programme was no longer given the time and resources it needed to succeed.[12]

The official line, especially among Western historians of the period, is that the explosion at Leipzig ended any realistic prospect of the Germans developing a successful nuclear bomb. It is certain that they were unable to develop a reactor of the type used by the Americans and their researchers. What is less clear is whether they were able to pursue alternative methods of developing atomic weapons which achieved at least a limited degree of success.

Susan Williams writes that: 'Leading German physicists were clear that, above all, it was the lack of uranium ore that had impeded German efforts to build a bomb.'[13]

Nuclear tests

'What if the enemy should get the atomic bomb before we did?' asked Winston Churchill.

Were his fears justified? Did the Nazis actually manage to manufacture an atomic bomb and even test it?

There is no doubt that the Germans were handicapped in comparison with the Americans, both in terms of the high quality of the scientists who were working on the Manhattan Project and of resources and unfettered testing options. The strong probability is that they were aware of these defects, and so followed a different path to try and achieve nuclear weaponry. It is possible that they achieved a degree of success, however, because eyewitnesses claim to have witnessed an atomic explosion and there is also evidence from declassified American documents that the Nazis carried out a successful nuclear test before the end of the Second World War.

More than one version of this claim exists, so perhaps the story that is supported by US documents is a suitable place to begin. Test pilot Hans Zinsser told Allied investigators that on a flight south of the German city of Lübeck:

> In early October 1944 I flew away 12–15 km (7.5—9 miles) from a nuclear test station near Ludwigslust (south of Lübeck).
>
> A cloud shaped like a mushroom with turbulent, billowing sections (at about 7,000 metres [23,000 ft])

stood, without any seeming connections, over the spot where the explosion took place. Strong electrical disturbances and the impossibility to continue radio communication as by lighting turned up.

Zinsser estimated the cloud as extending for around 6.5 miles (10.5 km) and mentioned what he called 'strange colourings', which were followed by a blast wave. This exerted 'a strong pull on the stick' [his cockpit controls in the plane]. His statement is recorded in the US National Archives in Washington.[14]

The American file reports on the 'investigations, research, developments and practical use of the German atomic bomb'. It concludes that German scientists were unable to achieve the same degree of success in nuclear weapons as the Allies, but that it is highly probable that they were able to test a nuclear warhead in 1944. Zinsser added, in his log read by the Allied investigators, that an hour later another pilot also observed the same phenomenon.

Other archival documents also report the Italian correspondent Luigi Romersa as having observed a different explosion from the ground, near the island of Rügen. Romersa had been sent by Mussolini to watch the 'new weapon' developed by German scientists and was instructed to report back on the results. This is his account of what he witnessed:

They took me to a concrete bunker with an aperture of exceptionally thick glass. At a certain moment, the news came through that detonation was imminent.

There was a slight tremor in the bunker; a sudden, blinding flash, and then a thick cloud of smoke. It took the shape of a column and then that of a big flower.

The officials there told me we had to remain in the bunker for several hours because of the effects of the bomb. When we eventually left, they made us put on a sort of coat and trousers which seemed to me to be made of asbestos and we went to the scene of the explosion, which was about one and a half kilometres (0.9 miles) away.

The effects were tragic. The trees around had been turned to carbon. No leaves. Nothing alive. There were some animals – sheep – in the area and they too had been burned to cinders.[15]

Ohrdruf incident

Rügen and Ludwigslust are not the only places that are claimed to have been Nazi testing sites for German atomic bombs. It is alleged that two further nuclear devices were detonated on 4 March and 12 March 1945 near the town of Ohrdruf in Thuringia. The tests allegedly killed more than 700 prisoners in the Ohrdruf concentration camp and it is said that the survivors received burns that were 'untreatable' and that they had suffered 'severe nosebleeds'. A local resident, Clare Werner, saw the explosion from a nearby hill and described it as follows:

It was about 9.30 when I suddenly saw something ... it was as bright as hundreds of bolts of lightning, red on the inside and yellow on the outside, so bright you could've read the newspaper. It all happened so quickly, and then we couldn't see anything at all. We noticed there was a powerful wind, then nosebleeds, headaches and pressure in the ears.[16]

The following day a local man working for an excavating firm was called upon by the SS to build wooden platforms to cremate the corpses of the prisoners. He described the bodies as being covered with 'horrific burn wounds' and also said that residents were complaining about spitting up blood and having severe headaches.[17]

Not only German witnesses but agents for Soviet military intelligence saw evidence of an atomic bomb. Reporting back to Russia about nuclear testing in the Ohrdruf region, they declared that:

> The Germans are in the throes of making and testing a new secret weapon, which has a large destructive force.
>
> The available bomb has a diameter of 1.5 metres (5 ft). It consists of interlocking hollow balls.

Another Soviet agent reported that:

> Communicated by our reliable source from Germany: the Germans have conducted two explosions in Thuringia with great force.[18]

Atomic bomb discovered

Did underground atomic bomb testing take place in the Chemnitz region of Germany? If amateur historian Peter Lohr was correct in his assumptions, Nazi atomic bombs were still present at the site when he investigated. He claims to have found traces of strange metal objects in an abandoned tunnel network built by the Nazis in the Jonas Valley near Chemnitz. In an interview with the German magazine *Bild*, he said, 'At least two of the objects are the Nazi atomic bombs.'[19]

There is no doubt that the Nazis forced slave labourers from Buchenwald to construct the tunnels in the region during the latter stages of the war, but their purpose has never been satisfactorily explained. Theories include the idea that they were intended to hide stolen treasures or were meant to provide a retreat for Hitler and other Nazi leaders. Lohr claims that they were designed as test sites for atomic weapons. He began investigating the site with ground-penetrating radar in 2012 and later confirmed his findings with 3-D modelling computer software. He described the site as containing an extremely large underground chamber holding five large metal objects. In his view, they clearly resembled atomic bombs.

> The metal has been deposited in the soil for 71 years. Eventually, it will decompose, and we will have a second Chernobyl on our hands.

He contacted the authorities with his concerns but they showed no interest. As Lohr put it: 'The only result is that I'm not allowed to continue my research.'[20]

Without independent verification, it is difficult to be sure how much weight to place on this additional claim for nuclear testing. Certainly, there is considerable testimony and evidence relating to the possibility of tests at Ohrdruf, Ludwigslust and Rügen.

Tiny bomb mystery

Whether or not there are unexploded atomic bombs still lying around in Germany, at least they are described as 'large', which is what most people would expect. However, a German exile in Argentina claims to have witnessed the destructive force of a pocket-sized atomic bomb. Adolf Freier asserts that on 4 March 1945 he witnessed an atomic bomb being tested at Ohrdruf. He goes into considerable detail about the testing of the device and perhaps the most surprising aspect of his claim is the small size of what he calls an 'atomic weapon'.

His account states that the bomb was only 100 g (3.5 oz) in weight, which is well short of the amount of plutonium necessary for a uranium atomic bomb. He also describes the blast as causing damage up to an area of 1.2 km (0.75 miles). Such extensive destruction with such a small device sounds implausible, but that rests on the assumption that the Nazi scientists were employing the same approach to nuclear physics as the Allies. It may well be that they had tried to do that but that the practical difficulties compelled them to adopt alternative strategies.

This inexplicably small amount of explosive charge has been one of the principal reasons for dismissing Freier's story as fantasy. Since the Manhattan Project required a critical mass of 50 kg (110 lb) for the uranium how could a mere 100 g have provided an effective nuclear bomb? Perhaps the financial and practical difficulties faced by Germany – and in particular their inability to develop a successful conventional reactor – might have encouraged them to look for cheaper and simpler ways of achieving nuclear capability. The idea that they chose instead to develop a uranium bomb, enrich it to the purity needed for weapon-readiness and then attach the warheads to their advanced rockets is quite plausible. Using such methods, it would be possible to create and launch an effective nuclear device. Using 'boosted fission' by adding deuterium and tritium to the atomic fuel would have enabled them to achieve a chain reaction. When we consider that Freier's account also mentions an underground heavy water plant – which of course would have contained deuterium and tritium – his story looks more credible.

An examination of the Ohrdruf site also confirms his claims. The area shows clear signs of a large explosion, with damage radiating from a common centre. Ohrdruf also has the highest level of background radiation in Germany, which is another significant point in favour of Freier's claim.[21] Can we say with certainty that this nuclear test took place? It is not possible to come to a definitive conclusion on the subject but it is certainly less easy to dismiss it as a fraud than it would have been some years ago. Far more is known now about Nazi nuclear physics than immediately after the end of the war, when many German scientists felt a need for concealment and evasion. There are also eyewitness accounts from multiple sources that claim an atomic test took place.

The evidence of radiation at Ohrdruf is hard to explain on any other basis than that of a nuclear weapon having been tested. More than that we cannot say, but it shows clearly that the Nazi atomic programme, like most of their scientific endeavours, was far more successful than has generally been believed.

Nuclear reactors

The existence of the Vemork heavy water plant is perhaps proof enough of the existence of nuclear reactors in Nazi Germany. It is difficult to think of another reason for its manufacture.

Certainly, both physics and chemistry followed entirely different lines under the Third Reich from those pursued by later Western countries. Examples of cold nuclear reactors come from two German scientists. The first of these, the chemist Paul Harteck, used dry ice to cool a nuclear reactor which avoided the problems of graphite reactors and was a cheap and effective solution.[22] Another process was described by the physicist Fritz Houtermans, who used methane to cool reactors. Both types of reactor also created large numbers of isotopes.[23]

Bomb delivery problems

One objection that has been raised to the idea of a successful Nazi nuclear device is the apparent absence of a suitable 'delivery platform' for an atomic bomb. The V-2 had the range to deliver it successfully but not the payload capacity to carry it and German aircraft were not capable of carrying such a heavy weapon long-distance, even unopposed. With the additional complications of enemy fighters and anti-aircraft weapons, they would have been unable to deliver the weapon to its target.

This raises the interesting question of the extremely small mass of the object supposedly tested at Ohrdruf. If somehow the scientists had managed to compress explosive power into a small object, the objections about the delivery platform difficulties would be overcome. It is also worth reminding ourselves that the Allied investigators were unable to explain the mysterious explosions at Ohrdruf.

The New York bomber

Could the London Blitz have been replicated in New York? Or, much worse, could an atomic bomb have destroyed America's biggest city at a stroke?

It has been suggested that at least one German aircraft was capable of carrying the payload to deliver an atomic bomb, even as far as the United States. It would have to be large because such a bomb could weigh several tons ('Little Boy', the Hiroshima bomb, weighed over 4 tons [3.63 tonnes]).

There are stories from both North Africa and the United States about an aerial battle over the coast of North Africa and the southern Mediterranean on 18 April 1943. This involved 46 US Curtiss P-40 planes shooting down over 100 German Junker transport aircraft escorted by 50 Messerschmitt fighters. There was a four-page story with illustrations about this attack in *Blue Bolt*, 6 January 1944, a comic book with artwork by Harry Ramsey.[24] (Although this edition of the comic book appeared in January 1944, the original drawings had been made in August 1943.)

Ramsey's rendition of the P-40s is orthodox, but the German bombers are presented as being six-engine aircraft. The only six-engine Junker was the Ju-390, which was first photographed during the invasion of North Africa in November 1942. This plane certainly had the range and capability of carrying a nuclear missile to its target. The problem is that the aircraft did not officially make its first flight until 20 October 1943. How then could Ramsey have drawn such an accurate picture of it before it had entered service? And how could it have been photographed in November 1942, a whole year before it first flew?

The most obvious answer is that the Ju-390 entered service much earlier than its first official flight and that it was fully operational at least a year before that date. In all probability, its

The Curtis P-40 was a single-engine, single-seat, all-metal fighter and ground-attack aircraft. Its shark mouth logo mimicked those found on certain Luftwaffe planes.

existence was a closely guarded military secret even among the Allies.[25] There is also a report of a Ju-390 flying from Europe via Canada and photographing defence plants in Michigan before flying back over the Atlantic on 28 August 1943. It supposedly passed directly above the Empire State Building in New York.[26]

Another report claims that in September 1944 a large six-engined plane with dark green and black paint crashed into the sea near Owl's Head Lighthouse in Maine. Three witnesses claim to have seen bodies recovered from the Penobscot River later that month which were then taken by the US Coast Guard to the Rockland station in Maine. One of them said he saw a body in a German uniform.[27]

These reports appeared to have been confirmed when some years later a female scuba diver found a radial aircraft engine lying on the bed of the sea. It was some way from the cliffs around the Owl's Head Lighthouse and she traced it back, together with some further wreckage littered on the sand, to the main fuselage of the aircraft from which it had come. One of the items she recovered was a plate with the following lettering:

RMZ WURKE Nb 135? 34 (Allgemeine)
JUNKERSMOTORENWERKE (Agts: Haan)
FWU WURKE Nb 135? 34
(Gbs: Fliegeroberstkommando Rdt.)[28]

If this really was a crashed German aircraft, what was the purpose of its mission? Was it engaged in a simple reconnaissance expedition or did it have more hostile intentions? An article by the *Daily Telegraph* in late 1945, which appeared two days after the bombing of Nagasaki, frankly admitted that the Germans had plans to bomb New York. It added for good measure that it was planned during World War One to attack New York with

Zeppelins and only the 'downing' of the fleet commander in an attack over England led to the abandonment of the idea.[29]

London was much closer to Germany and so it was far easier for German bombers to reach, but it was considerably better prepared for war than the United States and had excellent defences against aerial attack. America, however, even after Pearl Harbor, remained relatively undefended, particularly against attack from the air. New York had no defences against bombers penetrating its airspace and the idea of sending the Luftwaffe to bomb the city became extremely attractive to the German leaders.

The Ju-390 had a range of just over 6,000 miles (9,650 km). This was still short of the distance from occupied France to New York by around 1,200 miles (1,930 km), but the Germans considered plans for refuelling in the Azores region, held by neutral but pro-Nazi Spain. However, as the course of the war changed, Franco's neutrality became stronger and the use of the islands as a base to refuel German aircraft was denied.

The logistical difficulties, it is claimed, led the Germans to consider a daring plan to use a now defunct airfield at Sault Ste. Marie in Ontario, at the conjunction of Lake Superior and Lake Huron. By flying over Canada and into US airspace and refuelling at Sault Ste. Marie the Germans would be able to bomb New York and return to Germany. To further this purpose, German agents on the ground obtained two aviation fuel trucks.

The plan was for the plane to land on the disused airstrip and refuel there. A ship laden with fuel obtained in Canada would meet the trucks and offload the fuel and the trucks would then make their way through the forest to the waiting aircraft. German commandos would guard the area and the plane would land and refuel before taking off to make its return journey to Europe. Whether this was the plane that was said to have

----

crashed is uncertain but it does seem to suggest that a German aircraft might have been able to penetrate Canadian airspace and land and refuel successfully. That is a striking testament to the growing advances in German aviation during the war.[30]

Fizzle bomb

If the Nazi scientists did not quite manage to make a fission bomb, perhaps they were able to create a semi-fission, or 'fizzle', bomb? The size of the explosion created by this type of bomb falls far short of that of a full fission reaction, yet it is visually similar to a full atomic detonation. That would explain some of the test firing reports, where a tell-tale mushroom cloud was observed and radiation effects were experienced.

Yet did the man who led the German atomic programme also have enough knowledge to make a full fission bomb and if so did he deliberately hide that knowledge, as he said after the war?

Werner Heisenberg was not only the leading quantum physicist in the world, but he was actively backed by Himmler, with whom he had gone to school. His championing of relativity in spite of the unpopularity of Einstein's 'Jewish science' made him powerful enemies but Himmler consistently protected him.[31] Heisenberg was placed in charge of the German atomic energy programme and liaised with foreign physicists of the stature of Nils Bohr as well as leading German scientists. In 1946, when the war was over and he was trying to downplay his part in the Nazi regime, he admitted that in 1942 atomic scientists in Germany met to discuss ways to convert heat from uranium into water or steam, which remains clear and unequivocal testimony to the high priority given to nuclear research.[32]

The accepted view is that the Nazis failed in their quest to develop atomic power and atomic weapons. This view has been encouraged by the fact that Heisenberg adopted a variety of strategies to distance himself from the regime in general and his role in its atomic programme. He claimed at different times that he and his colleagues had been incompetent, that he was a secret anti-Nazi who had tried to sabotage the German atomic programme and, more plausibly, that the shortage of plutonium and the difficulties encountered when building effective nuclear reactors had made his task impossible.

Heisenberg was a Nobel Prize-winning physicist and the idea that he or his almost equally gifted colleagues were 'incompetent' is simply absurd. Nor do his anti-Nazi credentials pass serious scrutiny. His final excuse is more credible, but it is not necessarily a decisive objection to the idea that the Nazis developed a successful nuclear weapon.

There is no doubt that his attempts to create a nuclear reactor in Leipzig ended in disaster. The reactors caught fire and had to be put out, but it is arguable whether Heisenberg was attempting to produce a conventional fission bomb. It is even doubtful whether his reactor was designed for that purpose.

The surviving blueprints of German atomic research of the period show clearly that Heisenberg was not attempting to do that. His experiments were probably designed to create a 'fizzle' or semi-fission bomb. A fizzle bomb does create a nuclear explosion but it is not a complete fission reaction. It can disperse considerable radioactive fallout although its power is far short of that achieved by a fission bomb. The effects of a fizzle bomb are destructive and include the radiation following the dropping of the missile. In the circumstances of the war such a device could well have created sufficient terror to intimidate the Allies.[33]

The ultimate question is could Heisenberg have created a full fission bomb if he had really wanted to do such a thing? In 1945 the German scientists who had been involved in nuclear research were interned at Farm Hall, near Cambridge, where they were questioned at length about their work for the Nazis. After he had been given copies of the proceedings to read, Hans Bethe, a German and American scientist who was involved in the Manhattan Project, said: 'Heisenberg knew a lot more than I have always thought.'

Atomic engine

More evidence that the Nazis were successful in developing nuclear devices comes from Josef Ernst, a physicist debriefed by British intelligence after the war. Ernst states that a planned new jet fighter, the Messerschmitt P-1073, was designed to have three different types of engine. One was a BMW 003 petrol engine and the second ran on crude oil, but the third was powered by an 'atomic engine'. Ernst claims that it was manufactured at Camp Mecklenburg but that only a single prototype was developed, which was destroyed by the SS as they retreated.[34]

Further evidence comes from the *Heereswaffenamt* (Army Weapons Department). The director of research for the organization was the physicist Erich Schumann and Kurt Diebner was in charge of day-to-day research. Diebner was also responsible for atomic research within Germany and from 1942 onwards he persuaded the military to increase research and development for nuclear power. He also supervised the development of a uranium bomb at an underground location. Walter Dornberger, who directed the V-2 project, certainly wanted to win the war and hoped that atomic bombs or other 'wonder weapons' could still turn the tide in Germany's favour in spite of the increasingly difficult military situation in conventional warfare.[35]

It is also significant that it was these supposedly incompetent German scientists who were recruited by the Allies following the end of the Second World War. Both America and the Soviet

Union eagerly made use of their expertise in the development of their own nuclear programmes, military and civilian.[36]

How much did they really know?

Die Lesart – 'the version' – is the name Max von Laue gave to the 'agreement' between the scientists held at Farm Hall to put as much distance as possible between themselves and the Nazis. This sanitized account of their actions was the one that von Weizsäcker and, under his influence, Heisenberg, successfully presented to the world as sober fact. Heisenberg and von Weizsäcker both claimed in their interviews with the author Robert Jungk that they did not want the Nazis to possess nuclear weapons and therefore only pursued the atomic bomb half-heartedly. There is no doubt that both men were deliberately lying about their role in Nazi nuclear research.[37]

Given the circumstances immediately following the war, their evasiveness and downright untruths may have been understandable. All the same, the evidence clearly shows that the Nazi nuclear programme was far more advanced than Heisenberg and his colleagues were prepared to admit to their conquerors. Nor does the idea that the scientists – several of whom were fanatical Nazis – had no wish to develop a weapon that would help Germany win the war hold any credibility.

In 1945, many key German scientists were captured by the Allies and interned at Farm Hall in England, where the British intelligence services bugged their conversations. The transcripts of these tapes were not declassified until 1993, although aspects of them were leaked earlier. In at least some cases this 'leaking' was done with the deliberate intention of minimizing the complicity of the scientists in terms of their attitudes towards and actions under the Nazis.

The scientists held at Farm Hall were politically diverse with both Hahn and von Laue being anti-Nazi. Gerlach and Diebner, by contrast, were fanatical supporters of the regime. Heisenberg may not have been particularly politically minded, but he was a friend of Himmler's. The other scientists were largely non-political figures who simply wanted to pursue their research wherever it led them. The 'agreement' was drawn up at Farm Hall and drafted by Heisenberg though, in von Laue's own words, 'the leader in all these discussions was von Weizsäcker'. During a conversation at Farm Hall, von Weizsäcker, reacting to the news of the dropping of the atomic bomb on Hiroshima, remarked: 'I believe the reason we didn't do it was because all the physicists didn't want to do it, on principle. If we had wanted Germany to win the war, we would have succeeded.'[38]

This statement is difficult to reconcile with the fact that both Diebner and Gerlach were enthusiastic Nazis who certainly wanted Germany to win the war. It is also inconsistent with von Laue's cynical comment on 'the version', when he stated flatly that: 'I did not hear any mention of any ethical point of view.'[39] Clearly, the scientists at Farm Hall were trying to protect their own position and avoid any possibility of being tried by the Allies as war criminals.

The strong probability is that von Weizsäcker and Heisenberg were seeking to distance themselves from the Nazi regime and present an image of concerned but non-political scientists whose scruples led them to avoid pursuing nuclear warfare with full vigour. This cosy piece of reinvention is not supported by the facts and it is virtually certain that at least one nuclear bomb was successfully tested in Germany and another may have been used against the Soviets.

The reality is that the Nazi atom bomb project was relatively successful and with more time and resources it would have been every bit as destructive as the bombs that were dropped on Hiroshima and Nagasaki. Failure to develop an effective atomic bomb was neither inevitable nor the result of any lack of enthusiasm by the scientists working on its development.

Perhaps the final word on the subject should be given to Hitler. On 15 February 1945 his doctor, Erwin Gieser, met the Führer in the Chancellery air raid shelter. Gieser described Hitler as rambling, but said that he had boasted about a new weapon called an 'atom bomb' which would turn the tide of the war. Hitler declared that he would use the atomic bomb 'even if the white cliffs of England disappear into the water'. He then walked away and Gieser had no idea what he meant until the Americans bombed Hiroshima. That event also prompted Heisenberg to remark 'they have it too' to the other German scientists held captive with him by the British. There could hardly be a clearer acknowledgement that the Nazis had been equipped with the nuclear bomb and had almost achieved launch capability.

FOOTNOTES

1 Klaus Hentschel and Ann M. Hentschel (eds), *Physics and National Socialism: An Anthology of Primary Sources*, Birkenau, 1996

2 Otto Hahn, *My Life*, Herder and Herder, 1970

3 Lise Meitner and O. R. Frisch, 'Disintegration of Uranium by Neutrons: A New Type of Nuclear Reaction', *Nature*, 143 (3615): 239–240, 11 February 1939

4 Hentschel and Hentschel, op. cit.

5 Dan van der Vat, *The Good Nazi: The Life and Lies of Albert Speer*, Houghton Mifflin, 1997

6 Hitler's decree of 9 June 1942 can be found in Hentschel and Hentschel, op. cit.

7 Ibid.

8 Ibid.

9 Ray Mears, *The Real Heroes of Telemark: The True Story of the Secret Mission to Stop Hitler's Atomic Bomb*, Hodder & Stoughton, 2003

10 Nikolaus Riehl and Frederick Seitz, *Stalin's Captive: Nikolaus Riehl and the Soviet Race for the Bomb*, American Chemical Society and Chemical Heritage Foundations, 1996

11 Robert and Klara Döpel and Werner Heisenberg, 'Der experimentelle Nachweis der effektiven Neutronenvermehrung in einem Kugel-Schichten-System aus D2O und Uran-Metall'. In: Werner Heisenberg, Collected Works Vol. A II, Berlin, 1989

12 David Irving, *The Virus House*, William Kimber, 1967

13 Susan Williams, *Spies in the Congo*, PublicAffairs, 2016

14 Allan Hall, 'Did Hitler Have A Nuclear Bomb?' *Mail Online*, 23 February 2017; file APO 696 in the National Archives, Washington

15 John Hooper, 'Author fuels row over Hitler's bomb', *Guardian*, 30 September 2005

16 Klaus Wiegrefe, 'How Close Was Hitler to the A-Bomb?' *Der Spiegel*, 14 March 2005

17 Ibid.

18 Hall, *Mail Online*, art. cit.

19 Justin Huggler, 'German Pensioner Claims He Has Found Nazi Nuclear Bombs', *Daily Telegraph*, 18 May 2016

20 Ibid.

21 Joseph P. Farrell, *The SS Brotherhood of the Bell*, Adventures Unlimited, 2006

22 Irving, op. cit.

23 Jeremy Bernstein, *Hitler's Uranium Club: The Secret Recordings at Farm Hall*, Copernicus, 2001

24 *Blue Bolt*, 6 January 1944

25 The Wanderling, '1944 German Atomic Bomb', http://thewanderling.com/

26 Ibid.

27 Ibid.

28 Ibid.

29 *Daily Telegraph*, 11 August 1945

30 The Wanderling, website cited

31 Alan D. Beyerchen, *Scientists Under Hitler: Politics and the Physics Community in the Third Reich*, Yale, 1977

32 Thomas Powers, *Heisenberg's War: The Secret History of the German Bomb*, Knopf, 1993

33 Farrell, op. cit.

34 Ibid.

35 Hentschel and Hentschel, op. cit.

36 Annie Jacobsen, *Operation Paperclip: The Secret Intelligence Program that Brought Nazi Scientists to America*, Little, Brown, 2014

37 Robert Jungk, *Brighter Than a Thousand Suns*, Harcourt Brace, 1958

38 Bernstein, op. cit.

39 Farrell, op. cit.

CHAPTER EIGHT

THE BELL

As the Allies closed in on the Third Reich an increasingly desperate Hitler poured increasing resources into his *Wunderwaffen*. Although he was said to be ignorant of science – the concept of the atomic bomb 'strained Hitler's intellectual capacity', according to Speer – Hitler increasingly turned to his scientists for ever more advanced technology. 'I was familiar with Hitler's tendency to push fantastic projects by making senseless demands,' Albert Speer said later. But was the Nazi Bell a senseless demand or was it a serious and sophisticated device that could have made a major contribution to the German war effort?

There has been much speculation about the Nazi Bell. It was said by some to incorporate anti-gravity technology so advanced that it could have whisked its Nazi creators up to the moon, Mars and beyond. Others even thought that the Bell reappeared after the war as the UFO in the 1947 Roswell incident. How right or wrong were they?

Conception of the project

The Bell – *Die Glocke* – is the name given to an alleged Nazi secret project said to combine a bell-shaped flying saucer with nuclear power and 'scalar physics'. It is one of the most controversial of all the Nazi secret weapons claims.

The story of the Bell originated in the 1990s with the Polish writer Igor Witkowski. He claimed that a Polish intelligence officer showed him classified Soviet documents from the debriefing of a former SS officer called Jakob Sporrenberg. These described a mysterious project called *Die Glocke* which was allegedly tested underground at Der Riese under the authority of the notorious Hans Kammler.[1]

The Bell project was conceived in January 1942 and was known as *Die Tor* (the gate) until August 1943. At that point it was divided into two programmes, one known as *Laternenträger* and the other as *Chronos*. The overall code name for the project was *Charite Anlage*. It appears that the Bell was a nickname rather than an official title for the work on the programme.

Contributing scientists

Professor Walter Gerlach, one of Germany's leading nuclear physicists, was said to have been in technical charge of the project. He won a Nobel Prize for his work on the physics of gravity and was the head of nuclear research in the Third Reich during the latter stages of the war. His work on spin polarization was world famous. Some of Gerlach's other areas of expertise included ionized mercury and the transmutation of elements. This was nothing like the medieval pursuit of alchemy for it was firmly rooted in the exploration of the subatomic world. Gravity and spin were his primary areas of expertise and it is no surprise that both aspects of his skills are associated with the story of the Bell.[2] The range of individuals involved with the Bell is surprising.

Dr Elizabeth Adler, the mathematician, was one of the most unlikely of its members, as few female scientists or mathematicians were involved in serious work under the Nazis. She would have needed to be exceptional to be recruited to such a secret project.

Another puzzling aspect is that although she is said to have worked at the University of Königsberg (now Kaliningrad), there is no record of any Dr Elizabeth Adler as a former staff member there. Her role in the Bell was described as being concerned with 'a simulation of damping of vibration towards the centre of spherical objects'.

Many conspiratorial theories have been spun around the absence of her name but the truth is more prosaic. Either through a simple mistake or a process of deliberate disinformation her

Professors Otto Hahn, Walter Gerlach and Karl Friedrich von Weiszäcker arrive at the Palace Schaumberg in Bonn for discussions about nuclear power with the post-war German Chancellor, Konrad Adenauer. Discussions concluded with an announcement that West Germany would never produce nuclear weapons.

name has been wrongly given as Elizabeth Adler, but in reality she was a well-known and respected mathematician called Elisabeth Borman. Borman worked for Max Born, one of the leading German mathematicians and a man involved in many pioneering experiments in nuclear physics research. However, Born and Borman patronized a hotel in Stockholm known as the Adler Hotel and no doubt this is the source of the confusion.

Elisabeth Borman was an assistant to Gerlach and helped him measure 'the free path length of gas molecules'. All of these factors explain how and why she would be regarded as a suitable member of a team working at the cutting edge of physics, particularly one headed up by Gerlach. There is no 'mystery' about her presence in the team. It is nothing more than a case of misidentification. The attempts that have been made to put a conspiratorial spin on her name are simply mistaken.[3]

Hermann Oberth is one of the pioneers of rocket technology and a forerunner of spaceflight. The nature of his involvement with the Bell project is not clear, but there is no doubt that he went on what he described as a 'business trip' from Prague to Breslau between 15 September and 25 September 1944. He was accompanied on this journey by Herbert Jensen, Edward Tholen and the wrongly identified Dr Elizabeth Adler. We have seen already that her true identity was Dr Elisabeth Borman.

Prague was certainly home to many Nazi secret projects during the war and Breslau has often been suggested as the headquarters of research into flying disc projects. Oberth's main area of wartime activity was developing explosive devices and that is certainly highly relevant to the purpose of the Bell.

Kurt Debus was principally a rocket scientist. He worked with von Braun at Peenemünde and was involved in work for AEG on high electrical voltages. Debus developed a power supply unit at

AEG which provided over a million volts of electrical current. He is best known for his role in managing V-2 launches for the SS and later working for NASA on Apollo moon launches. He had expertise in the measurement of high voltage discharges.[4]

Dr Otto Ambros was a man whose official duties under the Third Reich included chairing a committee for chemical warfare and being a director of the Buna synthetic rubber factory at Auschwitz. Ambros was a chemist who developed a whole range of nerve gases under the Nazis which, along with a range of other poisons, he tested on inmates at concentration camps.

After the war he was arrested and tried and spent two years in prison as a convicted war criminal. He remained impenitent, unable to accept that his actions had been wrong in any way. Based on his history, it is not immediately obvious why he would have been involved with the Bell project.[5]

Herbert Jensen was one of the leading figures in the German nuclear programme. In 1938, he was working at Walther Bothe's Institut für Physik in Heidelberg and from 1939 to 1946 he was a teaching assistant to Bothe.

He worked on research into German atomic energy, in a project known as the 'Uranium Club', and his particular area of expertise was neutron scattering.

Jensen was involved in the construction of the *Uranmaschine* (nuclear reactor) B 8 (B-VIII) in Haigerloch and he and his other collaborators wrote up a report on their results.[6]

Karl Wirtz was a German physicist who worked with Fritz Boff and Erich Fischer on designing a horizontal layer reactor. In 1944 he became head of the experimental department at the Kaiser-Wilhelm-Institut für Physik. The Allies arrested him in 1945 and imprisoned him at Farm Hall.[7]

Otto Hahn was primarily a chemist, although he later became involved in physics. He worked in radiochemistry before the First World War, discovering thorium-228, which he named radiothorium. It was later discovered to be a radioactive isotope of thorium. Hahn discovered many entirely new elements and his reputation in the fields of chemistry and radioactivity increased. He worked with (and became a close friend of) the Austrian scientist Lise Meitner.

When Hahn discovered the phenomenon of nuclear fission it was Meitner who worked out the theoretical physics, leading to the earliest formulated theory of nuclear fission. Hahn's discovery of the fission of uranium was a turning point in nuclear physics. Meitner wrote later that 'it opened up a new era in human history. It seems to me that what makes the science behind this discovery so remarkable is that it was achieved by purely chemical means.' Hahn was recruited by the Nazis to work on uranium fission reactions and he discovered and isolated still more new elements and isotopes during this research.[8]

Kurt Diebner was one of the founder members of the 'Uranium Club' in 1939, which was interested in nuclear reactors and sustainable atomic chain reactions. Soon the *Heereswaffenamt* (HWA – Army Ordnance Office) took over the group and put them to work, with Diebner as the director of the Nuclear Research Council. Diebner quarrelled with both Heisenberg and Carl von Weizsäcker and was eventually replaced as director by Heisenberg. Nuclear fission experiments were conducted at the HWA test site in Gottow. These experiments produced an extremely high quantity of neutrons and represented a great advance on previous experiments in nuclear fission.[9]

Horst Korsching was a colleague of Karl Wirtz with particular expertise in the fields of thermal diffusion and determining the nuclear moment. He worked during the war on the separation of isotopes, under the direction of Diebner and Heisenberg.[10]

Carl von Weizsäcker began his research into nuclear energy by studying the stars. He and Hans Bethe discovered a mechanism for nuclear fusion in stars which was named after them, becoming the Bethe–Weizsäcker process.[11]

Once Hahn had discovered nuclear fission and Meitner had provided the theoretical basis for the phenomenon in physics, Weizsäcker recognized the potential of the process for creating nuclear weapons. He was soon recruited to the German atomic bomb project. His father held high office in the German government and Einstein warned President Franklin Roosevelt that 'the son of the German Under-Secretary of State, von Weizsäcker, is attached to the Kaiser-Wilhelm-Institut in Berlin where some of the American work on uranium is now being repeated'.

In September 1939 von Weizsäcker and his associates attended a meeting in Berlin, where the German nuclear bomb programme was instigated. Then in July 1940 he co-wrote a report to the army about producing atomic energy through refining uranium. He also suggested that plutonium would be suitable for the same process, in addition to playing a key role in an atomic weapons programme. In 1942 he applied for a patent for 'a process to generate energy and neutrons by an explosion'. Von Weizsäcker was one of the key figures in the German nuclear programme and pursued the quest for a nuclear bomb with vigour and dedication.[12]

Dr Eric Schumann worked with Dr Walter Trinks on designs for tactical nuclear weapons using uranium-233 for fission. They fired extremely hot lithium particles at 'targets' of beryllium and lithium deuteride. This resulted in a brief flurry of neutrons in what is known as a deuteron beam.[13]

Uranium-233 is a rare element and hard to separate and it is possible that at least one aspect of the Bell project was to produce uranium-233 for the scientists. Schumann and Trinks operated a laboratory near Peenemünde where experiments took place using superheated lithium with hollow charges.[14] This may be relevant both to the German nuclear programme in general and to the Bell in particular. We shall investigate the clear connection of the Bell with Nazi research into atomic energy and atomic bombs towards the end of this chapter.

Paul Harteck worked with Ernest Rutherford and was a chemist. He worked for the HWA from 1937 onwards and in 1939 he told the German War Ministry about the military importance of nuclear chain reactions. After 1940 he began researching the separation of uranium isotopes for the HWA and favoured the use of heavy water to moderate neutrons. Then in 1943 he proposed a new method of centrifugal isotope separation. This was developed under his direction by the Anschütz Company. Harteck also used the ultracentrifuge device to enrich uranium.[15]

Erich Bagge was a physicist involved in nuclear research. He developed an isotope sluice device to enrich the U-235 isotope content of uranium. The methods he employed were electromagnetism, thermal diffusion and centrifugal force.

Bagge's technique involved reacting uranium oxide powder with hydrochloric acid. The resultant compound was pumped through a sluice, which spun using centrifugal force at high velocities, scattering the heavier and non-fissile 238U to the edge of the device. The 235U was kept towards the centre of the centrifuge through electromagnetism which created intense heat, enabling the 238U to sink to the bottom while the 235U went to the top of the chamber. The compound gas with its enriched uranium 235U was then sluiced away from the upper levels. We shall see later that the work of Bagge in particular is highly relevant to the purpose and operation of the Bell.[16]

Tests of the Bell

The Bell was described as a device shaped like a bell which contained a liquid, possibly mercury, stored in two cylinders. The cylinders were spun in opposite directions and the Bell then emitted a blue light. Electrical circuits failed and people and animals in the vicinity were injured when this was done. The Bell's metal core contained a substance known as Xerum-525, which is said to be a compound of thorium, beryllium and mercury. By 1944 Germany had acquired the entire European supply of thorium but US intelligence could not provide an explanation for this behaviour. The mercury within the Bell was cooled with liquid oxygen and nitrogen.[17]

There were several tests of the Bell, each one taking place in an underground pool. The floor was covered with rubber mats and ceramic tiles covered the surface of the pool. After each test the mats were destroyed and the tiles were washed in strong disinfectant. When a test took place in an underground mine, the testing chamber was blown up after the completion of the experiment.

Once the Bell had been set up the power supply was turned on. Cameras and measuring devices were attached, after which various samples were placed in the chamber. These included plants, egg whites, milk, fat, various animals and even some concentration camp prisoners. Immediately prior to the tests the scientists and engineers put on protective clothing and retreated to a distance of 200 m (656 ft).

The effects of the Bell were extremely powerful. During the first series of tests carried out between May and June 1944, five of the seven scientists involved died. This led to the recruitment of a new team and a frantic determination to avoid a repetition of these events. Plants changed colour, becoming grey or pale, and curiously they lingered on for around a week after this transformation, before abruptly dissolving into a substance described as having the consistency of rancid fat. One can only imagine the effects on the scientists, to say nothing of the unfortunate concentration camp inmates, many of whom must surely have died.[18]

The Bell is alleged to have been tested at two sites, now both in Poland but before the war in Lower Silesia, then part of Germany. One test site was Leubus (today Lubiz) and the other Neumarkt (today Sroda Slaska). A third site is said to have been located at Schloss Fürstenstein (Fürstenstein castle) and a fourth was supposedly disguised as a coal mine in Waldenburg. All of these sites are in Lower Silesia.

Both the German government and two corporations provided funding for the project. The private backing came from AEG and Siemens. Near to the sites already mentioned was another location associated with the Bell, the Wenceslas Mine at Ludwigsdorf (today Ludwikowize). The Ludwigsdorf site was built with an extraordinary structure resembling a prehistoric henge. It was situated within a pool with ports through which electrical current passed.

Analysis of the henge by modern German physicists showed that it had clearly been subjected to radioactive bombardment from neutrons. They also discovered that the site had formerly been used as a device to accelerate ions. Clearly, the Bell project resulted in the emission of considerable amounts of radiation.[19] The Bell was not a 'spherical object', although Dr Elisabeth Borman was involved in 'a simulation of damping of vibrations towards the centre of spherical objects' relating to the project (see page 193). It also appears from the description that it did not vibrate.

Very high electrical charges appear to have been used during the experiments. The Bell also appeared to have created strong magnetic fields. There seemed to be considerable research into 'magnetic fields separation' and in some unexplained way vortex compression was also involved with its operation. The device, or at least parts of it, was spun to generate these electromagnetic effects.

Alchemy

The most significant aspect of all the properties ascribed to the Bell is that it emitted very powerful radiation. More bizarrely, there are stories that it was part of an experiment to turn mercury into gold. This points towards an interest in the pseudo-science of alchemy, which claimed to be able to 'transmute' base metals into gold. We will see shortly that this preoccupation is not only highly relevant to the Bell but may help to provide a clue about its true purpose.[20]

On a human level, the concentration camp prisoners detailed to work on the Bell and also serve as human guinea pigs came from the Gross-Rosen camp. This was a series of small camps in which almost half of the unfortunate inmates were young Jewish women who were fit enough to work, and so were spared the gas chambers. They were instead compelled to labour in appalling conditions with insufficient food, inadequate clothing, little shelter and virtually no medical treatment. Their involvement with the Bell shows that they were treated as 'laboratory rats' in the various experiments on the project. The Nazi scientists had no more regard for their well-being or survival than the politicians who ran the Nazi Party, or Hitler himself. They sacrificed them willingly in the pursuit of their 'scientific research'. Just as medical experiments, often of dubious value, were conducted on concentration camp inmates, so too the Bell represented yet another scientific 'experiment' with unwilling victims.[21]

High voltages

One of the most curious aspects of the Bell is the extremely high voltages used in its operation. This puts its study firmly in the field of plasma physics. Electrical current can create plasmas which in turn produce vortices called plasmoids. This leads to a plasma vortex which is virtually isolated from its surroundings, creating a local curvature of space.

The relationship between the Bell and plasma physics is conclusively demonstrated by the existence of a plasma trap exhibited at the Institute of Plasma Physics and Laser Microfusion in Warsaw. This plasma trap looked strikingly similar to the Bell and the device was shielded with rubber mats and ceramic tiles, as in the case of the Bell.[22]

These features, plus other aspects of the Bell's description, led Igor Witkowski to speculate that it was a large metal drum containing mercury, which was then accelerated until the mercury covered the walls of the drum. A high electrical charge was then passed through the device, accelerating the mercury ions and thus making them rotate. Witkowski believed that there were two 'spins', one centrifugal and the other centripetal. The combination of these opposing rotations, he believes, led to a compressed vortex which could counteract the effects of gravity. This fits in with some of the more extravagant claims of space travel that have been made for the Bell.

This is of course speculative and goes beyond the available evidence, resting on an assumption about the nature and purpose of the Bell's rotation. We will examine Witkowski's theories in more detail, and their subsequent development by Joseph Farrell, when we consider the various hypotheses about the truth behind the Bell project.[23] It is often claimed that Witkowski invented the story of the Bell and that there were no previous references to the project before his work. Another criticism is the claim that Witkowski's story was solely based on the unsupported testimony of Jakob Sporrenberg after the war was over.

Neither of these claims is correct. Unlike some stories about speculative Nazi technologies which appear to have been woven out of a mixture of rumours, half-truths, exaggeration and creative imagination, there are several sources predating Witkowski that refer to the Bell project.

Bell project sources

This does not mean that Sporrenberg, the original source for Witkowski's Polish informant, may not have been embellishing the truth, concealing or distorting and even perhaps simply misunderstanding aspects of the project. Nor does it mean that Witkowski's theories about the purpose and mode of operation of the Bell are correct. What it means is that the Bell, however misunderstood, distorted or exaggerated the stories about it became, represented a genuine Nazi secret weapons project. Impressively, the earliest reference to it comes as early as 22 April 1943, when Kurt Debus described the Bell in a document held in the US National Archives. A later reference to the project comes from Professor Meiczyslaw Moldovia, a former inmate of Gross-Rosen camp who worked in Fürstenstein castle and was one of the few survivors of the camp.

Another source is Dr Otto Cerny, who was working for NASA in the 1960s and told the story of the experiments to the father of Greg Rowe. Later, Rowe, who heard his father and Cerny talking about the project, recounted what he remembered to Henry Stevens, author of *Hitler's Flying Saucers*. Cerny described the device as a stone circle with a hoop inside, at the centre of which was the Bell itself. He claimed there was a concave mirror above it, through which it was possible to see behind. Cerny was one of the scientists working on the Bell who was recruited by the US as part of Operation Paperclip (a programme in which German scientists, engineers and technicians were recruited by the US after the Second World War). In his files he is described as an Electrical Installer on Supersonics. The Vienna technical university to which he was attached was part of an underground nuclear factory at Melk and a nuclear research centre at Zell am See.[24]

Richard Cremer, an engineer from Oberschönweide who was working on high voltages with AEG, was also associated with the Bell. Unfortunately for Cremer, he fell out with Walther Gerlach and was denounced to the Gestapo. The result was that he was sentenced to two years in prison. Cremer's imprisonment led Professor Carl Ramsauer of AEG to write an anguished letter to the Gestapo stressing his importance to the war effort and linking his work with the German atomic bomb programme.[25]

The development of the Bell is described in the autobiography of the physicist Rolf Wideroe. He produced a patent showing one sphere placed inside another with a common axle on which they spun. A vacuum was created to breed plasma within the empty chambers after which heated mercury vapour was bled into the aperture and spun, before powerful electrical currents were used to ionize the mercury. This made it glow and photons, colliding with electrons, then formed gamma X-rays. These rays stimulated the beryllium oxide and emitted thermal neutrons, which were then absorbed by the thorium and changed into protactinium. Wideroe described this device as the 'vortex tube' and though he mentioned one patent he had filed earlier patents for similar devices. In 1935 both the Swiss scientist Walter Dallenbach and the German Max Steenbeck applied for patents based on similar designs.[26]

An even earlier patent was applied for in 1934 by the Hungarian scientist Leo Szilard. His patent application was called 'improvements in or relating to the transmutation of chemical elements'. Szilard's patent application described the generation of radioactive bodies by bombarding elements with neutrons. He declared that 'such uncharged nuclei penetrate even substances containing the heavier elements without ionization loss and cause the formation of radio-active substances'. [27]

Anti-gravity research

After the Second World War Steenbeck worked for the Russians and tried to create a replica of the German Bell for the Soviets. The Russian version was known as the *Tokamak*.[28] The most generally accepted theory about the purpose of the Bell among its advocates is the notion that it represented a device that was designed to overcome gravity. Witkowski, Farrell and Stevens consider this its primary purpose and aviation writer Nick Cook seems to regard it as its principal function.[29]

Anti-gravity research has been pursued for well over a century and it is possible that Nazi scientists, many working at the edges of conventional physics and chemistry, might have devoted their time to such a project. Witkowski and Farrell urge in support of their theory the alleged expertise in gravitational physics of Walther Gerlach and Elizabeth Adler.

We have seen that Adler never existed and that her true name was Elisabeth Borman. She was a mathematician and not a physicist or a chemist, however, though she assisted Gerlach with many of his experiments, and Gerlach's alleged expertise in gravitational physics does not survive serious scrutiny. The evidence offered on behalf of that claim – the Stern–Gerlach experiment – does nothing of the kind.

These experiments would have yielded the same result irrespective of the presence or absence of gravitational features. Gravity was irrelevant to the Stern–Gerlach experiment so the claim that it represented proof of 'anti-gravity research' is simply mistaken.

One of the sources of the 'anti-gravity' aspects of the project may be deliberate lies told to his interrogators by Sporrenberg. He may also have given an exaggerated account of the Bell to the Soviets, including half-truths and downright fiction as well as the truth. Possibly he simply misunderstood the nature and workings of the Bell. The association of the Bell with anti-gravity may also be partly based on a mistaken association of the project with the work of Dr Ronald Richter, an Austrian-born German scientist, in the 1950s. We will examine this shortly when we deal with those aspects of the Bell that appear to relate to plasma physics. For the moment it is sufficient to say that while the Bell may have been involved in anti-gravity research such work was not its primary purpose and it did not represent a kind of new propulsion system based on the discovery of the use of anti-gravitational energy.

Plasma physics

Plasma physics was an area where Germany produced many eminent scientists and it would undoubtedly have been researched with a view to possible military applications. It has been claimed that at least some aspects of the Bell's operation were involved with plasma physics. During the 1950s Dr Ronald Richter worked in Argentina on experimental research designed to induce fusion using plasma shockwaves. He wrote to the United States during the same period applying for work on ramjet engines. Richter's claim was that plasma ramjets would not only allow fighter planes to take off and land vertically but would also dramatically reduce the fuel consumption of the aircraft by a factor of 20. Whether or not his claim was correct, no plasma ramjet has ever been observed.[30]

Farrell and Witkowski link the plasma physics aspects of the Bell with other claims. These involve aspects of theoretical physics that are not simply controversial but are also generally regarded as belonging to the realm of pseudo-science. They begin by making an initial unsubstantiated assumption, suggest ways in which this might have led to certain results and formulate a new hypothesis on the basis of what is primarily speculation. Farrell, for instance, begins with a possibility – that Nazi scientists managed to discover a particular type of subatomic particle mutation. He goes on to suggest, in his own words, that:

> If they coupled this idea to spin-cohered or charge-polarized plasma, it is a very short step to the idea that the way to maximize the phenomena would be via a large aggregate of matter – in a plasma – and to further stimulate that activity through pulsing of a radioactive substance.[31]

Farrell has 'added' an 'if' to a 'maybe' and then a further 'perhaps' and on the basis of these assumptions formulated a theory with little evidence to support his claim. It is highly doubtful that this is a correct account of the workings of the Bell. There is only a single fact in Farrell's paragraph, that the transcripts from the bugged conversations of captured German scientists held by the British suggest they employed unorthodox methods in their research into nuclear power. Whether these were the principal methods employed is more dubious.

On the basis of a few fragmentary and ambiguous remarks, which may have been at least partly designed by the scientists to mislead their captors, Farrell erects a theory more in keeping with science fiction than sober fact. He declares confidently that:

> All these factors suggest that the Germans were experimenting with the very structure and fabric of matter, energy, gravity and space-time with the Bell,

and for various purposes: propulsion, weaponry and energy supply.[32]

Farrell is probably correct to suggest that plasma physics played a part in the operation of the Bell. He is on less certain ground when he attempts to assimilate the device to anti-gravity research. His thoughts on the possible connection of the Bell with the transmutation of elements miss the most obvious area of application, atomic energy. He weaves together a mysterious pattern rather than drawing the logical conclusion, that the process of 'transmutation' and the Bell in general involved nuclear physics. Beginning from a series of unusual aspects of the story that are still capable of being explained within an orthodox scientific framework, he leaps to the science fiction notion of nuclear-powered saucers. When a simpler and more logical theory is available and the evidence supports that explanation, suggesting a more speculative idea to account for the project seems a mistaken approach.

Nuclear project link

Otto Hahn was one of the leading scientists working on the German nuclear programme. He was involved in experiments with the Jewish scientist Lise Meitner, using photo fission techniques to examine the properties of neutrons and modify elementary particles. Meitner was the senior partner in their research and even when she fled to Sweden in 1938 Hahn continued to rely heavily on her expertise. He communicated with her by airmail throughout the war and had no idea that she was passing on every scrap of information he gave her about the German nuclear programme to the Allies. Under Operation Epsilon, Meitner simply told MI5 everything she learned from Hahn. It is only fair to add that Hahn was certainly not a supporter of the Nazis and was particularly hostile to their anti-Semitism. He may even have deliberately communicated with Meitner in the hope that she would betray his secrets to the Allies.[33]

Ronald Richter, whom we have already come across regarding his work in the field of plasma physics, conducted several experiments in 1936. He used arc furnaces to try and produce lithium for U-boat batteries and discovered that when he injected deuterium into the lithium plasma it produced radiation. Richter monitored the temperature within the furnace by using the level of radiation produced by the process to determine its level. These experiments were undoubtedly factors in his recruitment in 1942 to the Bell project. It was his connection with radioactivity rather than any alleged 'anti-gravity' experiments that would have recommended him to the German authorities.[34]

There are three fragmentary passages of conversation recorded in the Farm Hall transcripts that may refer to the Bell. One is a brief exchange between Bagge, Diebner and Korsching discussing 'work on the uranium engine'. Korsching responded scornfully that 'there won't be any money in it', adding 'if you invent something like artificial rubies for the watchmaking industry, you will make more money than with the uranium engine'.

The second conversation took place between Hahn, von Weizsäcker, Harteck, Wirtz and Diebner. They were discussing the separation of isotopes to obtain uranium-235. Hahn believed it was 'absolutely impossible' to do so except 'with mass spectrographs', adding that 'Ewald [Heinz Ewald] has some patent'. Diebner then responded, 'there is also a photochemical process'.[35]

Heinz Ewald developed a mass spectrometry method of working with electromagnetic isotope separators for U-235. He established the correct values for the isotope ratios of Cu (copper) and from them derived a new value for the atomic weight of Cu. Then in 1942 Ewald proposed an isotope separator and a prototype was constructed near Bad Saarow to the south of Berlin. Hahn was presumably referring to these researches and experiments by Ewald when he mentioned 'mass spectrographs' as being the only way to separate isotopes.[36]

Farrell is more interested in the 'photochemical process' mentioned by Harteck. He interprets this as a reference to achieving nuclear reaction through cold fusion. It is ironic that earlier in his book he pointed out the true significance of the 'artificial rubies' remark by Korsching, yet ignored its relevance to the 'photochemical process'.[37] What these German scientists were describing, in a guarded and elliptical way, is not cold fusion, scalar physics, anti-gravity propulsion systems or flying saucers – nuclear powered or otherwise. They are simply discussing methods of separating uranium isotopes. What they call the 'photochemical process' involved the use of laser technology to bombard the atoms and achieve this separation.

Lasers are monochromatic, which means that a single species can be isolated and 'excited' in an isotope mixture. By altering the nuclear mass, changes can be produced in the level of vibration, electronic frequency and rotation. Deuterium substitution can shift the vibrational frequencies of atoms beyond their normal range. Firing lasers at particular wavelengths changes the behaviour of atoms and this was clearly the 'photochemical process' referred to by Harteck.

It is overwhelmingly clear that the Bell was not concerned with anti-gravity, flying saucers or similarly exotic technology. The probable purpose of it was in relation to Nazi nuclear projects. It may have been used to breed either uranium or plutonium or it might have been designed as a particle accelerator.

Protactinium harvesting

Thorium was mined in the Erzgebirge at the very site where the Bell project was located. The Auer company was also refining thorium into metal and after the D-Day landings all the stocks of thorium in France were evacuated to Germany. According to Dr Ernst Nagelstein, a German scientist, Hahn was using thorium (or possibly uranium) to develop an atomic bomb.[38] Erich Schumann attempted to develop hollow miniature nuclear weapons using specially devised high-speed explosive and Schumann and Trinks applied for a patent for a hollow charged atomic bomb using U-233 as its fissile core.

Thorium may be transmuted into uranium-233 if it is bombarded with protons at a particular energy rate. The process is known as photo fission and it can also successfully breed plutonium-239 from uranium-238.[39] Thorium-232 can also produce protactinium-233 if an artificial neutron source is used to breed it. After 27 days protactinium naturally degrades into uranium-233, of a quality and purity sufficient to use in nuclear bombs.

When uranium-233 is produced by deriving it from the waste of a reactor it is not always sufficiently pure. It is often contaminated by uranium-232 if the thorium is bombarded by another neutron. This makes it far more dangerous to handle than when dealing with weapons grade plutonium.

Heisenberg may have subscribed to 'the version' for public consumption but there is clear evidence, particularly from the record of a speech found in the archives of the KGB, that he also proposed the 'harvesting' of protactinium for the purposes of creating a nuclear bomb. This speech was given by Heisenberg at the Harnack Haus conference in July 1942. Even in the Farm Hall transcripts, where he was trying to distance himself from the Nazis, Heisenberg again mentioned that process as one of the three possible ways of obtaining the necessary fissile material to make an atomic bomb.[40]

The three methods of obtaining the fissile material for nuclear weapons are to enrich uranium, to reprocess plutonium from waste in a nuclear reactor, or to harvest protactinium to create a bomb. Enriching uranium and reprocessing plutonium are well known but the third method, the harvesting of protactinium, seems to have slipped out of the public domain.

The Bell appears to have been devised to obtain protactinium. From the accounts of the design and working of the Bell, it sounds as if it was a heavy particle accelerator used to breed protactinium from thorium.

A particle accelerator uses electromagnetic fields to propel charged particles to close to the speed of light but contain them within beams of light.

When uranium-233 is derived from nuclear reactor waste it is often contaminated but the use of a particle accelerator prevents this from happening. The greater rapidity of the process means that the level of contamination is extremely low and it is therefore as safe as weapon grade plutonium.

Hermann Bucher, chairman of AEG during the war, told a spy for the American OSS (the forerunner of the CIA) that his company was involved in developing a heavy particle accelerator for the German nuclear weapons programme. The process employed used mercury to create collisions between photons and electrons and thereby free thermal neutrons. It then utilized a device that was surrounded by a concave mirror of beryllium, which reflected the neutrons back into thorium oxide at the core. The machine generated this X-ray plasma in orbit around an axle which spun two frequency-phased contra-rotating drums.

Bucher's spy for the Americans told them that Heisenberg and the Swiss engineer Walter Dallenbach worked on the Bell at a secret facility. The OSS also received information from an engineer called Nagelstein, who described Hahn's laboratory and told them that they were using thorium to create uranium for a nuclear bomb.[41]

Gerlach, the head of the Bell project, was in charge of the German atomic bomb research. Once more we see how clearly the Bell was not some kind of exotic flying saucer using anti-gravity but an integral part of the Nazi nuclear programme. When the evidence is considered beyond the mystification, sensationalism and flights of fantasy, a clear hard core of truth emerges. The story of the Bell does not involve anti-gravity craft, a nuclear-powered flying saucer, an exotic form of population or any of the other functions which have been attributed to the project.

Instead, the Bell project used a particle accelerator to obtain uranium of sufficiently high purity to be used in the Nazi atomic bomb programme. The Germans saw its military potential and were not as far behind the Americans in its development as is generally believed. Had there been more time available to them, a greater amount of resources for them to develop the project and more favourable military conditions, it is highly possible that the exceptional group of German scientists would have successfully produced a fully functioning atomic bomb. That is the true secret at the heart of the story of the Bell and it is impressive and frightening enough without overlaying the sober truth with unnecessary myths and legends.

FOOTNOTES

1 Igor Witkowski, *The Truth About the Wunderwaffe*, Books International (European History Press), 2003

2 Bernstein, op. cit.

3 Rob Arndt, 'Die Glocke' (1945), http://bell.greyfalcon.us/Glocke.htm/

4 Michael Neufeld, *The Rocket and the Reich: Peenemünde and the Coming of the Ballistic Missile Era*, Free Press, 1995

5 http://www.wollheim-memorial.de/en/otto_ambros_19011990/

6 Mark Walker, *German National Socialism and the Quest for Nuclear Power, 1939–1949*, Cambridge University Press, 1993

7 Ibid.

8 Klaus Hoffmann and Otto Hahn, *Achievement and Responsibility*, Springer, 2001

9 Bernstein, op. cit.

10 Walker, op. cit.

11 George Gamow and J. Allen Hynek, 'A New Theory by C. F. Von Weizsäcker of the Origin of the Planetary System', *The Astrophysical Journal*, 101: 249

12 John Cornwell, *Hitler's Scientists*, Viking, 2003

13 Mark Walker, *Nazi Science: Myth, Truth and the German Atomic Bomb*, Perseus, 1995

14 Bernstein, op. cit.

15 Ibid.

16 Rainer Karlsch, *Hitler's Bombe*, Deutsche Verlags-Anstalt GmbH, 2011

17 Farrell, op. cit.

18 Witkowski, op. cit.

19 Ibid.

20 Farrell, op. cit.

21 https://www.gross-rosen.eu//

22 Farrell, op. cit.

23 Witkowski, op. cit.

24 Farrell, op. cit.

25 Ibid.

26 Ibid.

27 Ibid.

28 John Wesson, *Tokamaks*, Oxford University Press, 2011

29 Farrell, op, cit.; Stevens, op. cit.; Nick Cook, *The Hunt for Zero Point: Inside the Classified World of Antigravity Technology*, Broadway Books, 2003

30 Joseph P. Farrell, *Nazi International: The Nazis' Postwar Plan to Control the Worlds of Science, Finance, Space and Conflict*, Adventures Unlimited, 2009

31 Farrell, *The SS Brotherhood of the Bell*, Adventures Unlimited, 2006

32 Ibid.

33 Hahn, op. cit.

34 Farrell, *Nazi International*

35 Bernstein, op. cit.

36 Ibid.

37 Farrell, *SS Brotherhood*

38 https://sites.google.com/site/naziabomb/home/nazi-bell-project-background/

39 http://www.abovetopsecret.com/forum/thread445406/pg7/

40 Paul Lawrence Rose, *Heisenberg and the Nazi Atomic Bomb Project, 1939–1945: A Study in German Culture*, University of California, 1998

41 Ibid.

CHAPTER NINE

EXPERIMENTAL SCIENCE

The Nazis explored a number of avenues, such as free energy, death rays and perhaps anti-gravity devices in their quest for supremacy. However, one of the towering scientific achievements of the 20th century, Einstein's general theory of relativity, was condemned as 'Jewish physics', as was his earlier theory of special relativity. The latter was particularly relevant to the Nazis' search for ever more deadly weapons because it was here that he described the equivalence of mass and energy, which he expressed in the famous equation $E=mc^2$. This could be seen as making the atomic bomb theoretically possible, though he did not consider such a possibility at the time.

Even quantum physics was for a time branded 'Jewish physics', but the Nazis soon recognized its value to their cause.

Theory of relativity

When the Nazis came to power in 1933, the prevailing attitude to science was that German scientists led the world, so why contaminate German science with incomprehensible theories such as the theory of relativity or quantum mechanics?

The theory of relativity assumes that the speed of light is constant and nothing can travel faster than light. It also claims that the fundamental bedrock of the universe is a four-dimensional curved space-time and because of the nature of this space-time continuum the laws of motion do not apply to it. And it asserts that all action in the universe is rigidly determined and that distant objects cannot influence local objects in an instantaneous way without some intermediate medium. Rooted as they were in classical physics, many of the leading German scientists of the time found it impossible to accept Einstein's conclusions, particularly as his 1905 theory of special relativity had ignored the idea of an ether.

This rejection of Einstein went even further when a number of leading German physicists, through a movement called *Deutsche Physik*, declared that while 'Aryan physics' was rooted in reality and was based on experimentation, 'Jewish physics' was based on abstruse theory that could not be related to experience. According to them, physics should be 'German' and 'Aryan' and not Jewish.

Quantum physics

Quantum physics presents a universe where the determinist approach favoured by Einstein is incompatible with the behaviour of atoms. It has been proved that distant objects can and do influence other objects without the need for any kind of mediation. Instead of the predictable and ordered world that Einstein described, quantum theory reveals a world of randomness and unpredictability. This is an enormous move away from Newtonian physics, where particles have definite properties at all times. Einstein never accepted that quantum physics was true and many quantum physicists rejected relativity.

Like relativity, even quantum physics was seen for a while as a 'Jewish science'. This was partly because it was a theoretical science, which the 'Aryans' detested, and partly because some of its proponents were linked to the Jewish faith. For instance, Max Born, the 'father of quantum mechanics', was originally Jewish, even though he had converted to Lutheranism, and Werner Heisenberg, one of the key pioneers of quantum physics, was also a supporter of relativity. He was not a Jew, but this made him a 'White Jew' in the eyes of the *Deutsche Physik* brigade.

However, it was soon seen that quantum physics was essential to the development of nuclear weapons and nuclear energy. Even so, Hitler was never totally at ease with what he saw as 'Jewish science' and some believe that this was one of the reasons why the Nazis did not develop a fully functioning atomic bomb.

The ether

There are many different theories concerning the nature of the ether. All agree that it fills the universe, but some regard it as a substance and others as a field of force or as a vortex of energy. In the 19th century, the 'substance' view of ether was the dominant ideology. Ether is particularly associated with the idea that the forces of gravity and electromagnetism require a material medium, ether, to transmit their energy. Isaac Newton, Georges-Louis Le Sage, Lord Kelvin and Bernhard Riemann all proposed different models of a mechanical gravitational ether.

Ether was believed to be the medium in which light and electromagnetic radiation was transmitted and this model was referred to as 'luminiferous ether'. There was almost universal agreement among scientists that such a medium not only existed but must exist. This remained the dominant view in science until the end of the 19th century and the beginning of the 20th.

At the end of the 19th century, the famous Michelson–Morley experiment attempted to detect the ether by tracing the Earth's motion through the ether, but it failed completely. This sent shock waves through the scientific community and a range of new theories were proposed to explain this failure.

Joseph Larmor proposed the notion of the ether as a magnetic field in motion precipitated by the acceleration of electrons. His theory marked a break with the classical view of the ether as a static medium.

James Clerk Maxwell remained committed to the existence of the ether but admitted that 'we have now to show that the properties of the electromagnetic medium are identical with those of the luminiferous medium'. Maxwell attempted to show that the ether was a medium occupying the space between one body and another in which one acted upon the other.

Hendrik Lorentz and George FitzGerald constructed an elegant and complex mathematical model which attempted to explain the failure to detect the motion of the ether by proposing the mechanism of length contraction. Their theory has never been refuted but with the growing acceptance of the new relativistic ideas of Einstein it fell out of fashion.

Einstein began his scientific work as a firm believer in the existence of the ether. In spite of the failure of the Michelson–Morley experiment to detect it, as late as 1895 he stated that 'the velocity of a wave is proportional to the square root of the elastic forces which cause its propagation, and inversely proportional to the mass of the ether moved by these forces'.[1]

However, when he formulated the theory of special relativity Einstein provided an explanation that was just as satisfactory mathematically as that of Lorentz and FitzGerald but did not require the existence of the ether as a support. At this stage in his career, Einstein still believed that relativity needed the presence of some kind of medium and initially rejected the conclusion that others drew from his calculations, which was that no such medium existed. Later he changed his mind and went so far as to say that if the ether could be detected then his theory of relativity would be wrong. However, his rejection of the idea carried more weight than this modification of his position and gradually the notion of the ether was abandoned by most scientists.

Schappeller's ether theory

With the Nazi regime in power, open advocacy of Einstein's theory was discouraged. Teaching it was still permitted, but increasingly his theory was mentioned without refererence to its originator. 'Aryan' names were used instead of Einstein's, but in essence relativity theory was still taught and used even under the Nazis. In spite of that, those scientists who totally rejected it continued to work and research. Following an entirely different path, they produced a considerable body of developed science and engineering with practical applications and consequences.

Karl Schappeller postulated a different formulation of ether physics from the classical exponents of the theory. The ether was seen in his theory as more than simply a necessary substrate for the universe. Unlike the 19th-century ether physicists, who saw the ether as particles of solid matter, Schappeller and his disciple Cyril Davson saw it as representing the activity of waves.

The ether physics of Davson and Schappeller was different from the classical conception of the ether in other ways. They believed that there was a counterpart to the orthodox Second

December 1930: Albert Einstein stands on the platform at Bahnhof Zoo, Berlin with his wife and friends; he's on his way to America for the second time. In 1933, Einstein and his wife were returning to Germany via Belgium when they learned their cottage had been raided by the Nazis and their sailing boat confiscated. Einstein promptly renounced his German citizenship in Antwerp, so the Nazis sold his boat and converted his cottage into a Hitler Youth camp.

Law of Thermodynamics. This states that increasing heat leads to an increase in randomness and disorder – entropy, to use the technical term. The admitted tendency of things to deteriorate in the presence of increased heat following the Second Law of Thermodynamics was, according to Schappeller and Davson, countered by a principle of what they referred to as 'reverse thermodynamics'. Their claim was that an increase in cold creates order and reduces the effects of entropy.[2]

Zero-point energy

Schappeller then built a device to demonstrate this principle. Cold was not seen by Schappeller and Davson as the simple absence of heat – it was regarded as the cold discovered at the centre of a vacuum in space. In this environment, there is little or no matter to be measured, but in spite of the absence of material substance in deep space there is abundant energy.

Light, electromagnetism, radiation and what is often called 'zero-point energy' all exist in an environment of absolute cold. This was the type of energy regarded by Schappeller as being the energy of the ether.

Absolute zero is, of course, extreme cold and if a disc made of conductive material is placed in an environment at that temperature and an electrical charge is applied, the current will flow and rotate endlessly around the disc. There is no loss of energy at absolute zero. The interstellar cold of zero point stores the energy in a state that Schappeller himself described as 'latent magnetism'.

He believed that out of this latent magnetism a process of excitation could turn the energy into matter and into electromagnetic energy. Zero-point energy – the cold ether – was in his view the origin of both matter and energy. Davson explains it paradoxically by saying 'primary heat is composed of cold energy'.[3]

The fact that it not only seemed to work but offered the promise of 'free energy' attracted the attention of successive German governments. In 1930, the device was taken over and developed by an organization of the German Weimar Republic, the *Reichsarbeitsgemeinschaft* or Reich Works Association (RAG). One of its aims was to make Germany self-sufficient in energy production and the Schappeller device seemed to provide the answer. The somewhat grandiose hope of the RAG was to link a number of Schappeller devices together to entirely eliminate the electrical grid.

The concept remained a dream by all appearances, but it is known that Karl Schappeller actually met with SS Reichsführer Heinrich Himmler in Vienna in 1933. At some point Schappeller, who had been born in a poor-house, became rich enough to live in a castle. Whether his wealth was due to the sale of his device is not known.

Vril

In 1871 the novelist Edward Bulwer-Lytton published a novel called *The Coming Race*, in which he described a subterranean master race, the Vril-ya. This race of beings had access to a liquid energy source called Vril, which could do many things such as heal, destroy or power machines. Although all of this was pure fiction, it fired the public's imagination and found expression in many forms. A curious fact is that the name of the meat extract Bovril is an amalgam of 'bovine' and 'Vril', thereby implying that Bovril was some sort of power food.

The Nazi Party had its roots in an organization called the Thule Society and it is said that some of its senior members subscribed to the notion of a troglodytic master race, just as Bulwer-Lytton had described. Some Nazi mystics are even said to have gone in search of the elusive Vril.

The idea of Vril is linked to Schappeller's formulation of ether physics. One of the differences between classical ether physics and Schappeller's variant was that the concept of inanimate matter was virtually dispensed with in his version.

Schappeller believed that living organisms are moulded by a creative life force – Vril, as the authors of the RAG booklets openly called it. Michael Watson, a physicist who was an acquaintance and disciple of Davson, stated 'this process is life force and the reverse of the Second Law of Thermodynamics. It is the vital force: Vril.'[4]

Other scientists and thinkers were also working along these lines in the 1920s. Ehrenfried Pfeiffer collaborated with Rudolf Steiner and asked Steiner a direct question:

> Is it possible to find another force or energy in nature, which does not have in itself the ductus of atomizing and analysis but builds up, synthesizes? This force must have the impulse of life, of organization within

itself as the so-called physical energies have the splitting, separating trend within themselves. Does such a force or source of energy exist? Can it be demonstrated? Could an altruistic technic be built upon it?

Steiner replied rather ambiguously: 'Yes, such a force exists, but is not yet discovered.' He identified it with the ether but added that 'it is formative ether force because it is the force which relates the form, shape, pattern of a living thing, growth'. Steiner declared that the use of this force could be 'the source of a new energy'.[5]

Energy into matter

The ether was regarded by many eminent scientists as the way in which energy became converted into matter. Sir Joseph Thomson declared that 'all mass is mass of the ether; all momentum, momentum of the ether; all kinetic energy, kinetic energy of the ether'.[6] This kind of attitude, combined with over 200 years of scientific progress, which had taken place under a belief system that regarded the ether as a necessary substrate for the universe, helps us understand why there was such opposition to Einstein's theories. Einstein's views were not only new, radical and complicated but they described a universe bearing little or no resemblance to what we experience in ordinary life. In addition, they required the abandonment of a whole network of belief on the basis of which successful scientific progress had been achieved. One of the fiercest opponents of relativity was Nikola Tesla.

Death rays

'Death rays' have long featured in science fiction stories and military powers such as the Nazis have often aspired to own such weapons. They are said to have been working on two projects during the Second World War, which apparently did not come to fruition.

Several independent scientists claimed to have produced working death rays and have even tried to sell their ideas to interested governments. One such was Nikola Tesla, who was one of the great names in science. An inventor, a physicist, a man who created and sent the first wireless transmissions, the man who discovered the fundamental principles of applying electromagnetism to practical use – his achievement is outstanding. Because of his stature as a scientist perhaps his claims can be taken more seriously than most.

Teleforce weapon

Tesla examined a Van de Graaff generator and declared that it could function as what he referred to as a 'teleforce weapon'. The media picked up his idea but employed the terms 'death ray' or 'peace ray' rather than Tesla's carefully chosen name. Tesla claimed it could function either as an anti-aircraft weapon or against soldiers on the ground.

He stated that his teleforce weapon could produce energy in free air rather than requiring a vacuum. It was capable of generating exceptionally high electrical charges and of amplifying and intensifying the forces developed by the mechanism and it contained a method of creating electrical repulsion, which was the 'particle gun'.

Tesla made remarkable claims about the concentrated beams of particles his gun could emit, the distances it could operate over and the catastrophic effects it could have on enemy forces. It would cause 'armies to drop dead in their tracks'.

In 1937, Tesla said flatly that he had 'built, demonstrated and used' the teleforce weapon. His few surviving records of the device show its workings are based on small tungsten pellets being accelerated through high voltage. He claimed that it was a 'superweapon that would put an end to all war'.[7]

Tesla wrote an article in 1937 called 'The New Art of Projecting Concentrated Non-Dispersive Energy through the Natural Media'.

This described an open-ended vacuum tube with a gas jet seal to allow the escape of particles, a way of supercharging particles to a level of millions of volts and a way to create and direct non-dispersive streams of particles using electrostatic repulsion. He then approached the United States, the United Kingdom, the Soviet Union and Yugoslavia to persuade them to adopt his device.[8]

Of all the nations he approached the one that showed the highest degree of interest in Tesla's weapon was the Soviet Union and in 1937 he presented his ideas in New York City to a Russian 'front organization', the Amtorg Trading Corporation. Two years later, tests of his device were made in the USSR and Tesla was paid $25,000. No further development of his idea is known to have taken place. On the other hand, his 'teleforce' device is strikingly similar to later charged-particle beam weapons developed during the Cold War by both the Americans and the Russians.[9]

In an earlier description of teleforce from 1934, Tesla wrote:

> My apparatus projects particles which may be relatively large or of microscopic dimensions, enabling us to convey to a small area at a great distance trillions of times more energy than is possible with rays of any kind. Many thousands of horsepower can thus be transmitted by a stream thinner than a hair, so that nothing can resist. The nozzle would send

concentrated beams of particles through the free air,
of such tremendous energy that they will bring down
a fleet of 10,000 enemy airplanes at a distance of 200
miles from a defending nation's border and will cause
armies to drop dead in their tracks.[10]

Tesla's concept of 'teleforce' was first mentioned on 11 July 1934
by the *New York Sun* and the *New York Times*. They described
it as a 'peace ray' or 'death ray'. Tesla disliked the term, but his
own language was partly to blame because he had referred to his
device as being a 'death beam', although he then tried to clarify
his position, stating that:

This invention of mine does not contemplate
the use of any so-called 'death rays'. Rays are not
applicable because they cannot be produced in
requisite quantities and diminish rapidly in intensity
with distance. All the energy of New York City
(approximately two million horsepower) transformed
into rays and projected twenty miles, could not kill
a human being, because, according to a well-known
law of physics, it would disperse to such an extent as
to be ineffectual. My apparatus projects particles.[11]

Tesla was strongly anti-Nazi and did not offer his weapon to
the Third Reich. On the other hand, particularly as some of his
research was already in the public domain, it is highly probable
that the Germans at least researched and considered his weapon
and tried to develop a form of the device themselves. It is also
possible that during the two years of the Nazi–Soviet Pact,
when both nations were co-operating extensively, the Russians
may have let their German counterparts know the results of
their own tests in 1939.

Energy from the ether

A perfectly rational, non-relativity-based approach to science under the Nazis often led to some surprising results. Ether physics had 'worked' well for 300 years and many scientists saw no reason to believe that it would not continue to do so.

One area in which research was keenly pursued was the idea that faster than light travel might be possible. Scientists also viewed electromagnetic force fields as a promising avenue of approach and much work was undertaken in both areas. In the area of atomic research, Nazi scientists pursued three separate lines of exploration. One method was to disintegrate atoms using a high potential vacuum tube with a huge electric current passed through it, another was the more conventional approach followed by the British and American scientists, and the third was the attempt to produce nuclear fusion.

A diagram alleged to represent a power plant for flying discs shows two devices, one of which is a central sphere bearing a striking resemblance to Schappeller's spherical device. This unit was started by an initial electrical charge which allowed the device to 'gather' energy from the surrounding area. That part of the machine, according to Davson, exemplified 'reverse thermodynamics'. The electric generator surrounding the sphere rotated, gathering electrical energy to feed 'Tesla pancake coils' on the outer walls. Both parts of the device functioned as a single system where each of the components attracted one another and through that process circulated energy continuously. The electromagnetic radiation from the sphere 'levitated' the device, while the pancake coils steered it.[12]

The RAG pamphlets speak of some of the intended uses for this machine. In *Vril* the writer declares:

> The new dynamic technology will, in the future, be able to drive electric locomotives and automobiles

without the manufacture of costly armatures and everywhere through connection to the atmospheric voltage network. New types of aircraft with magneto-static power devices and steering, which are completely crash and collision proof, could be built for a fraction of the cost of today's aircraft.[13]

The firm conviction that the ether was a medium from which it was possible to derive limitless amounts of energy found considerable favour with the new Nazi regime. Germany was economically still in a depression and needed to find any means necessary to reduce its costs, particularly in areas such as fuel or energy where it was hugely dependent on imports for most of its production.

Davson believed that the use of ether physics could be made a means of revolutionizing transport. He says:

The new technique will not concern itself with the air as a supporting medium, but wholly with the ether. The glowing magnetism core in the Stator must be able to vary its intensity according to the height at which the ether ship is to be raised and supported whilst in transit. This is the basis of the new principle for ether ships.[14]

Anti-gravity devices

There has been considerable speculation about possible Nazi research into anti-gravity. The notion of gravity possessing a 'negative pole', as some advocates describe it, is not entirely impossible, at least in theory. It is said by some that a huge number of Operation Paperclip documents are still being kept secret and that among them is information relating to German anti-gravity experiments. Conspiracy theorists have it that the 'flying disc' that crashed at Roswell, New Mexico in 1947 was an anti-gravity device based on German research acquired by the US after the war.

Electromagnetic field of force

Einstein, attempting to formulate his own theory of gravity, came up with what he called the principle of the 'uniqueness of free fall', sometimes known as the 'weak equivalence principle'. This principle states that an electrically neutral body falls independently of its structure or constituent parts while an object that was electrically charged and spinning would behave in a different manner from a neutral body.

The lines of force around a magnet do not simply run from pole to pole but also in a spiral and in opposite directions. If two magnets are held in place by a rod set through holes in the centre of each magnet, they will not touch. As the Earth is itself a 'magnet' with a huge magnetic field, it might be possible in principle to construct an electromagnetic field of force that was somehow able to 'oppose' the pull of the Earth's gravity, and so 'levitate' at that point.

The theoretical possibility of constructing such a field of force exists but the practical difficulties of creating a device capable of overcoming gravity on any level that could provide sufficient energy for a vehicle are immense and in particular the problems of stabilization for such a craft would be extraordinarily hard to solve.

In classical Newtonian physics, gravity operates within a static field. Einstein predicted, on the basis of his general relativity theory, that mass in motion would generate a gravitational force that behaved in a non-Newtonian manner. The gravitational field generated in this way has been referred to as a 'protational field'.[15]

It has been suggested that gravitational fields with negative mass would intercept gravity and thus enable it to be overcome.

The Meissner effect, found in superconductivity, describes two bodies repelling one another which again has been claimed as a possible method of overcoming gravity.[16]

Types of anti-gravity device

There are six fundamental types of anti-gravity device that have been suggested, all operating on slightly different principles. Mechanical devices are alleged to work on the basis of high-speed rotation; acoustical devices are supposed to operate by using vibration to alter the interaction of nuclear particles with the force of gravity; electromagnetic devices using extremely high voltages have been proposed; microwave devices are said to employ high-frequency electromagnetic fields; solid state anti-gravity devices supposedly work by a shielding mechanism within the atomic structure; and nuclear anti-gravity devices are said to work by altering the interaction of gravity with the atomic nucleus, rendering Newton's Third Law inoperable, and so overcoming gravity.

All of these theories are, at least theoretically, possible. The problem is that there is insufficient evidence that such experiments took place to any significant extent and no evidence that they were successful. The Bell, which has been claimed as an example of successful anti-gravity research, was, as we saw in the chapter that dealt with that particular Nazi project, simply part of the German atomic energy programme and not some kind of exotic anti-gravity craft.

The Black Sun

An even more bizarre suggestion is the concept of *die Schwarze Sonne* – the Black Sun. This is said to be the cold, imploding vortex proposed by Schappeller and Schauberger which is supposed both to gather mass and to generate hidden cosmic rays. The Black Sun, according to this theory, is what astronomers now call a 'black hole'. It draws in mass and energy and generates huge quantities of radiation at its outer edges. A black hole, it is claimed on this interpretation, contains both centripetal and centrifugal force, the centrifugal vortex perhaps opening on to another dimension where limitless energy flows like a tsunami.[17]

The Black Sun was also the symbol of the Vril Society, a mystical organization that met in Vienna. They were said to derive their power from the Black Sun, which was an infinite beam of light that exists in anti-matter. The Nazis also appear to have taken the concept of the Black Sun on board, because a similar design was incorporated into a floor at Wewelsburg Castle. This was the physical and ideological headquarters of the SS, presided over by its leader, Heinrich Himmler. Another example of the Black Sun design was found on a Second World War bunker memorial to Bismarck.

Albert Einstein first predicted black holes in 1916, by means of his theory of relativity, and anti-matter theories were developed during the 1920s, and so would have been known to German scientists and researched by them. Experiments based upon anti-matter would have been founded on the notions of other dimensions, parallel worlds or a 'many worlds' theory. This idea has often been proposed by quantum physicists as a possible explanation of the often bizarre behaviour of subatomic particles.

Anti-matter particles are not the same as the 'contents' of a black hole. They consistently display certain characteristics, in particular an absence of negative mass, while within a black hole both matter and anti-matter are contained. Both positively and negatively charged particles exist within a black hole.[18]

The notion that research into this kind of area might have taken place under the Third Reich is not impossible or even implausible. Although there is no evidence to suggest that machines constructed along these principles may have been produced or even tested, we know that by the end of the war the Nazis were researching a number of devices that only needed a little more time to perfect. Perhaps the evidence of their research was destroyed along with the Third Reich.

FOOTNOTES

1 http://www.straco.ch/papers/Einstein%20First%20Paper.pdf/

2 Cyril W. Davson, *The Physics of the Primary State of Matter*, Elverton Books, 2016 (first published 1955)

3 Ibid.

4 Farrell, *SS Brotherhood*

5 Alla Selawry, *Ehrenfried Pfeiffer: Pioneer of Spiritual Research and Practice*, Mercury Press, 1992

6 George Paget Thomson, *J. J. Thomson, Discoverer of the Electron*, Thomas Nelson, 1964

7 'A Machine to End War', *Liberty*, February 1937

8 O'Neill, op. cit.

9 Bernard Carlson, *Tesla: Inventor of the Electrical Age*, Princeton University, 2013

10 'TESLA, AT 78, BARES NEW "DEATH-BEAM"; Invention Powerful Enough to Destroy 10,000 Planes 250 Miles Away, He Asserts. DEFENSIVE WEAPON ONLY. Scientist, in Interview, Tells of Apparatus That He Says Will Kill Without Trace', *New York Times*, 11 July 1934

11 Ibid.

12 Davson, op. cit.

13 https://archive.org/details/TaeuferJohannesVrilDieKosmischeUrkraft193025S._201612/

14 Davson, op. cit.

15 Robert A. Freitas Jr., *Xenology: An Introduction to the Scientific Study of Extraterrestrial Life, Intelligence and Civilization*, Xenology Research Institute, 1979

16 Wayne M. Saslow, *Electricity, Magnetism and Light*, Academic Press, 2002

17 Joseph P. Farrell, *Reich of the Black Sun: Nazi Secret Weapons and the Cold War*, Adventures Unlimited, 2004

18 Kitty Ferguson, *Black Holes in Space-Time*, Franklin Watts, 1991

CHAPTER TEN

THE HUMAN COST

After the D-Day landings on 6 June 1944 the people of Britain were starting to relax, thinking the war was almost over. Then suddenly, on 13 June 1994, the first of Hitler's V-1 flying bombs hit east London. The exact spot is today marked with a blue plaque. After that date, more than 9,000 V-1s would be aimed at London and other parts of south-east England.[1] Many of them would be brought down by fighter planes and anti-aircraft guns, but a total of 6,184 people would be killed by the 'doodlebugs', as they were called, and 17,981 would be seriously injured.

William Joyce, otherwise known as 'Lord Haw-Haw', made the purpose of the bombardments clear in his broadcast of 24 June 1944:

> For nine days, with very little interruption, the V-1 projectiles have been descending on the British

capital. May I remind you, the name V-1 has been given to them officially. 'V' is the capital letter of the German word 'Vergeltung', which means 'retaliation'.

The 'doodlebugs' appear

The nature of the V-1's operation added to the destruction with a blast wave rippling out from the epicentre of the explosion, creating a 'push and pull' effect. At the point of impact buildings hit by the bomb were demolished. Areas with densely packed terraced houses were particularly affected with as many as 20 houses collapsing and solid brick walls splintering into fragments of powder.[2]

Even at some distance from the epicentre of the blast, roofs, window frames and walls were ripped apart to expose the house and its contents to the weather. At a greater distance from the blast, windows were blown out and slates were blown off the roof. Hundreds of homes were damaged – many beyond repair – and with the summer of 1944 being cold and wet, repairing the properties was difficult and took many months. Londoners shivered and found themselves homeless overnight.[3]

The range of the devastation inflicted by the V-1 extended for between 400 and 600 yd (365–550 m). Those unfortunate enough to be directly impacted by it were blown to pieces or crushed by falling masonry. Many people were trapped underneath collapsed buildings and had to be dug out of the debris, but not all of those who were rescued survived.[4]

In the early stages of the V-1 campaign, many people were injured by flying glass. As the attacks became more frequent and predictable, Londoners took cover, which reduced injuries from splinters of glass but increased the number of victims crushed and buried in their ruined homes. Tens of thousands received minor injuries and many lost friends or family members and saw the destruction of their homes and possessions.[5]

The initial V-1 assault was inaccurate and relatively ineffective. Ten were launched but five of them crashed. One landed in a field near Swanscombe in Kent and left 'a large corona of metal fragments surrounding a three feet deep (1 m) crater shelving to a wide saucer'.

The first successful V-1 bomb landed on 13 June 1944 on Grove Road in Bethnal Green. At 4.00 a.m., the air raid sirens sounded and ack-ack gunners began firing at a single aircraft flying faster than anything they had ever seen. Bursts of flak cut through the air as the civil defence team tried to shoot down the intruder but they failed to hit it.

Suddenly the engine cut out and the aircraft dived to the ground, exploding into a giant fireball. The Grove Road flying bomb killed six people, injured 28 and made over 200 homeless, but wartime censorship attributed the casualties to a German bomber that had been successfully shot down by anti-aircraft units. Four other V-1s landed that day, but Grove Road was the only target successfully hit.[6]

Within six days, 499 people were killed, 2,051 were injured and 137,000 homes were damaged as 72 of these unknown craft hit London. In one severe incident on 18 June 1944, a V-1 struck the Guards' Chapel in the Wellington Barracks on Birdcage Walk, where a large congregation of military personnel and civilians had gathered for morning service. It scored a direct hit, destroying the roof, the pillars and the supporting walls. Falling rubble crushed many of the congregation, killing 121 and seriously injuring 141 others. The chaplain conducting the service was among the dead as were several senior officers in the British army, an American army colonel, five musicians from the Coldstream Guards band and the band's musical director.

Medical teams and rescue crews rushed to the scene to find complete destruction. An ARP assessment estimated that there were between 400 and 500 casualties. The rescue crews found it difficult to work as the debris from the fallen walls and roof had trapped many people. Even the doors to the chapel were blocked, so the rescue crews had to approach from behind the altar and medical teams were forced to scramble between the walls to administer first aid and give drugs. It took 48 hours to free all of the survivors from the wreckage. R. V. Jones was working nearby at MI6 and noted that 'the whole of Birdcage Walk was a sea of fresh pine leaves, the trees had all been stripped and I could hardly see a speck of asphalt for hundreds of yards'.[7]

This devastating incident forced the government to relax its censorship and newspapers were allowed to announce officially that the Germans had developed a new and deadly secret weapon. The V-1s soon acquired the nickname of 'buzz bombs' or 'doodlebugs', but this grim gallows humour was a desperate act of defiance against a weapon for which, at least for the present, there seemed no adequate defence.

Before long Londoners listened intently to every sound in the air, for they knew that the V-1s hummed as they approached, before cutting out and landing. The novelist H. E. Bates described the effect of the plaster dust they created: 'It covered streets and roofs and trees, it covered people with a ghastly great bloom that was like the mask of death.'[8]

Anti-aircraft units were hitting a tiny proportion of the V-1s, which were being launched at the rate of 50 a day. Lieutenant-General Pile described how 'in the districts where they fell, our troops were refused cigarettes in the local shops and even denied access to restaurants'.[9]

After four years of intensive bombardment by the Luftwaffe, the early spirit of resolution had turned to one of fear and resentment. The V-1 campaign had been aimed at reducing the people's already brittle will to fight and it was starting to produce the desired effect. Government ministers visiting bombed-out areas were heckled and booed and even Churchill faced hostile crowds. Herbert Morrison, the Home Secretary, urged a mass evacuation of much of the population of London and by late July 229,000 had already left and busloads of children were carried to railway stations and sent to other parts of the country, mainly to the north and west. Morrison believed that the threat posed by the new weapons might lead to a mass exodus that could not be controlled and that 'whether their anger will be directed solely against the enemy may be doubted'.[10] His fears were justified because official estimates of 'private' evacuees from London reached a total of 1,450,000.[11]

Air defences reorganized

Britain began reorganizing its air defences to counter the new and unexpected threat. Along the southern coast of England a total of 1,600 anti-aircraft batteries were deployed. Initially, the speed of the missiles was too great for the anti-aircraft gunners to bring their weapons to bear, but this problem was overcome when proximity-fuse shells and radar-controlled batteries were introduced. The effects were dramatic and by the end of the summer three-quarters of the V-1s launched against Britain were destroyed by ack-ack fire.

Most V-1s were launched from sites in northern France and around 9,000 of them were sent against England over a period of 80 days. At the height of the campaign of terror over 100 rockets a day were landing in Britain. Later, other launch sites were used, such as Liège and Antwerp in Belgium and even Germany.

The death and devastation inflicted by the V-1s was immense, but it could have been worse if there had been fewer technical problems with the missile and British air defences had been weaker. Two days after the first V-1 was launched, an RAF Mosquito shot down a 'doodlebug' in mid-air and soon Spitfires, Mustangs, Tempests and Meteors were deployed to intercept the missiles before they landed. Over 1,000 V-1s were successfully destroyed in flight by the RAF. Some pilots even managed to approach close enough to the bomb to tip it off its intended course by nudging it with their wingtips. Others dived on them from a high altitude and strafed them with their guns.[12]

The technical difficulties that the Germans had encountered with the V-1s also assisted the British. The poor quality of the flying bombs' guidance systems meant that as many as 2,000 of them crashed shortly after they took off. In the end, only 20 per cent of them successfully reached their target.

Their effectiveness was further reduced because of a controversial decision by British intelligence to supply the Germans with misinformation. Their agents then passed on this false data to the crews of the Luftwaffe, who programmed their missiles using inaccurate co-ordinates which meant that they fell short of the centre of London. The decision was hotly disputed among some circles of the British government, as the result was that the London suburbs rather than the city centre were hit by the weapons. However, the consensus was reached that, although this would still lead to considerable death and destruction, the overall effect would be to reduce casualties as the suburbs were less heavily populated than the inner London districts.[13]

The V-1s' reign of terror ended at last in October 1944, when the launch sites in France were overrun and captured by Allied troops. For a while, sites in Germany continued to pound Belgium with the missiles and then they too fell silent. The end of the V-1 menace brought no respite from German missiles as almost immediately the more dangerous V-2 ballistic missiles began to attack London; they did not cease their aerial assault until March 1945.[14]

V-2 – death without warning

The threat posed by the V-2s was known about before they were launched and Churchill was so alarmed about their possible effect on morale that he began suggesting 'unrestricted use of chemical and biological weapons' against the Germans.[15]

Mustard gas, phosgene and anthrax were the weapons he advocated, a move that was strongly supported by Herbert Morrison. Detailed plans to gas millions of Germans were drawn up and Churchill tried to exert pressure on his colleagues and senior military personnel to begin using these tactics. He faced opposition not only from within his Cabinet but also from his military advisers. The JPS (Joint Planning Staff) drew up a report suggesting that not only would it inflict numerous civilian casualties – estimated by them at around ten per cent of the population – but it would also lead to devastating air raids on Britain, which would shatter the already fragile morale of the civilians.

The JPS report concluded that the use of anthrax would 'make a material difference to the war situation' but that the bacteria would not be ready to deploy for another six months. It added: 'We do not believe that for us to start chemical or biological warfare would have a decisive effect on the result or the duration of the war against Germany.' The secretary of the committee finished the report by declaring that, while the Germans might be able to keep control even under chemical attack, 'the same cannot be said for our people'. In the face of the rejection of his plans by the military experts, Churchill reluctantly abandoned the idea.[16]

The first V-2 rocket hit London on 8 September 1944. Travelling at up to 3,500 mph (5,630 kph) and with a range of

200 miles (322 km) it was the world's first long-range combat-ballistic missile.

Although Londoners could not hear the V-2 coming, because of its speed the sound of the rocket rushing through the air could be heard after it had landed.

A ten-day period saw many casualties and much destruction before there was a sudden lull in the attacks. On 3 October, they began again, after the Germans had moved their rocket units to The Hague, following the failure of the Allied assault on Arnhem.[17]

The V-2s were expensive compared with the V-1s and never achieved the same scale of devastation as their predecessors, but their psychological impact was greater. The standard Anderson air raid shelters were useless as the rockets easily penetrated them and only the deep Tube stations provided safe havens. The far greater degree of penetration achieved by the V-2 and its more concentrated focus made it a deadly weapon. When it landed, the V-2 left a crater that could be 60 ft (18 m) wide and 16 ft deep (5 m). From September onwards, a series of what the newspapers referred to as 'gas explosions' occurred in London and it was not until 10 November that the government finally admitted that they were the result of the new German missiles.[18]

Public anger

Most of the V-1s landed in south London but the V-2s were mainly directed against east and north London. Ilford received the highest number of hits with 35 of the missiles striking this relatively small town. The response of the people was anger, particularly against the government. They knew the Germans were losing the war and the incautious promise by a government minister that 'the Battle of London is over' roused fury. During the Blitz, there had been a sense of community spirit and defiance, but after four years of war and bombardment that had been replaced by a feeling of war weariness and a sense of anger that the German bombardment could not be stopped.[19]

The V-1 campaign had led to thousands of people becoming homeless. Tens of thousands of those who had endured damage in the V-1 raids still had no running water, no windows and no roofs to their homes and the repair works dragged on for months. People were also falling ill and influenza was striking down large numbers of the population.

Victims of a V-2 flying bomb are helped from their wrecked house, London 1944.

In Brixton, women prayed in the street for the war to end and the morale of the people was at its lowest ebb as the rockets continued to hit London.[20]

Although there were many incidents involving V-2s, two stood out from the rest. The first took place on 25 November 1944 at the New Cross Woolworth's store, when 168 people died. It was a Saturday, when the store was crowded with shoppers. As they swarmed around in search of the few goods that were available in wartime, a rocket scored a direct hit.[21] Then on 25 March 1945 a V-2 landed on Hughes Mansions in Stepney, killing 145 of the building's occupants. Ironically, the Stepney missile was the last V-2 to be launched against England.[22] A total of 5,475 people were killed in Britain by the V-2s and 16,309 were wounded. Most of the rockets fell on London but Norwich and Ipswich were also hit.[23]

There is no doubt that the V-2 created a sense of terror and anger greater than any previous bombing raids. A real sense of defeatism began to emerge and it is hard not to feel that if the rockets had been launched earlier in the war they might have succeeded in breaking the spirit of the British people.[24] Albert Speer believed that insufficient time and resources had been put into developing the rockets and that if they had been prioritized earlier the course of the war might have been different.[25]

Slave labourers

England was the principal target of the V-2s but other countries also suffered their onslaught. Belgium was the hardest hit country on mainland Europe with a total of 1,664 fatalities; 1,610 in Antwerp, 27 in Liège, 13 in Hasselt, 9 in Tournai, 3 in Mons and 2 in Diest. There were 76 deaths in France; 25 in Lille, 22 in Paris, 19 in Tourcoing, 6 in Arras and 4 in Cambrai. And 19 people were killed in Holland, all at Maastricht. Even in Germany 11 people were killed by the V-2, at Remagen.[26]

Most V-1s were made by slave labour at the Gerhard Fieseler Werke factory in Kassel. Some were also made at the infamous Camp Dora (Mittelbau-Dora concentration camp), which was also responsible for the production of the V-2.[27] These weapons of mass destruction were made by concentration camp prisoners in an underground complex known as the Mittelwerk. The inmates of Camp Dora were compelled to work under horrific conditions and life expectancy was short. Out of 64,000 prisoners at Camp Dora 26,500 died, 15,500 of them in the camps and a further 11,000 when the SS was frantically evacuating the facility and simply murdering prisoners in cold blood. Most of the inmates were Russian, Polish and French and some of the most notorious images of concentration camp survivors come from the prisoners in Camp Dora and the wider Buchenwald complex.

First of all the prisoners were forced to enlarge and complete the underground tunnel system. They worked and lived in appalling conditions, having to eat and sleep inside the tunnels. Their beds were bunks in the cross tunnels and they were plagued by lice and insanitary conditions as well as the fumes from the blasting work and gypsum dust. There was no running water and they worked in 12-hour shifts, the blasting continuing 24 hours a day. Not surprisingly, typhus, tuberculosis and dysentery were rampant and, as their rations were meagre, malnutrition and even starvation led to many unnecessary deaths. They had to work on top of 30 ft (9.1 m) scaffolds with picks to widen the tunnels. Often a prisoner would simply fall from the scaffolding with exhaustion and hunger and be killed and he was immediately replaced with another unfortunate inmate. The corpses were then loaded up and taken to the crematorium at Buchenwald.

The equipment from Peenemünde was installed in the tunnels once this preliminary work was completed. Prisoners carried the materials and parts for the rockets by hand, using block and tackle, skids pulled by groups of inmates and hand-carts to transport them along the railway lines.

In October 1943, only 7,000 inmates were at Camp Dora. By January 1944 this figure had risen to 12,000 and by February 1945 to 19,000. Other subcamps were built, employing more slave labourers, and the death rate there was even higher than at Camp Dora. An official SS report states that in August 1943 a total of 17,535 inmates arrived at the camp and by April 1944 the prisoner figures were 11,653. That meant 5,882 inmates had disappeared from the records – 2,882 of them had been recorded as dying on the job and the others as having been transported to 'other camps'. Those who were 'transported' were too weak to work and the likelihood is that they were simply exterminated. A total of nearly 6,000 deaths in seven months gives an idea of the inhumane conditions and utter neglect of the welfare of the slave labourers.

Some prisoners tried to sabotage the rocket programme as much as possible, but that was a dangerous course of action. Not only was the penalty for sabotage death, but the SS would 'punish' such acts with group hangings to deter other prisoners. Horrific though the deaths inflicted by the V-2 were, more people were killed manufacturing the weapon than when it hit its target.

When the Allies eventually liberated Camp Dora, they found over 2,500 corpses, along with the emaciated and desperate survivors. Battle-hardened soldiers could not believe the scenes of horror they encountered when they discovered the camp.[28]

The astonishing advances in science, technology and particularly in weapons of war should not blind us to the human cost of their development. Civilian lives were lost on a scale never previously seen. Most of the weapons, aircraft and the parts needed to make them function were produced by slave labour.

We can admire the skill, ingenuity, futuristic and visionary nature of the accomplishments of the Nazi scientists and engineers and the way their work laid the foundations of the space programme. On the other hand, scientific and technical advances should benefit humanity while those developed under the Third Reich merely served the purpose of destruction.

Underground weapons facility

What has been described as 'the biggest secret Nazi weapons factory' was discovered near the small Austrian town of St Georgen an der Gusen. Complete with a network of tunnels that hid mass graves, the subterranean complex stood in 75 acres (30 ha) of land and its development was personally supervised by Himmler. It stood close to the B8 Bergkristall factory and relied on slave labour from Mauthausen concentration camp; some 320,000 inmates were worked to death on the premises.

Everybody knew about the factory, but the existence of the tunnels was uncovered by Austrian film-maker Andreas Sulzer backed up by ground-penetrating radar. Sulzer discovered that the project manager was the notorious SS General Hans Kammler, who was in charge of a number of advanced Nazi weapons projects, including the development of the V-2 and the revolutionary Me 262 jet fighter which was built on site.

As historian Rainer Karlsch explained, 'They wanted to equip the A4 [V-2] missile, or more advanced rockets, with poison gas, radioactive material or nuclear warheads.' At this point in the war, the Nazis were increasingly desperate to beat the Allies to the world's first atomic bomb and change the course of history.

FOOTNOTES

1 Angus Calder, *The People's War: Britain 1939–1945*, Jonathan Cape, 1969

2 http://www.flyingbombsandrockets.com/V1_into.html/

3 Ibid.

4 Ibid.

5 Ibid.

6 http://www.eastlondonhistory.co.uk/v1-v2-rocket-attacks-east-london/

7 R. V. Jones, *Most Secret War: British Scientific Intelligence 1939–1945*, Hamish Hamilton, 1978

8 H. E. Bates, cited in: Christy Campbell, *Target London: Under Attack from the V-Weapons*, Little, Brown, 2012

9 Sir Frederick Pile, *Ack-Ack: Britain's Defence Against Air Attack During the Second World War*, Harrap, 1949

10 Campbell, op. cit.

11 Bob Ogley, *Doodlebugs and Rockets: The Battle of the Flying Bombs*, Froglets, 1992

12 John Christopher, *The Race for Hitler's X-Planes*, The History Press, 2013

13 Ewen Montagu, *Beyond Top Secret Ultra*, Coward McCann & Geoghegan, 1978

14 Alexander Ludeke, *Weapons of World War II*, Parragon Publishing, 2007

15 Campbell, op. cit.

16 Ibid.

17 Benjamin King and Timothy J. Kutta, *Impact: The History of Germany's V-Weapons in World War II*, Da Capo, 2003

18 Ibid.

19 http://www.flyingbombsandrockets.com/V2_intro.html/

20 Norman Longmate, *Hitler's Rockets: The Story of the V-2*, Hutchinson, 1985

21 http://ww2today.com/25-november-1944-168-dead-as-woolworths-obliterated-in-v2-rocket-attack/

22 http://www.flyingbombsandrockets.com/V2_maintextc.html/

23 http://www.wrsonline.co.uk/the-v2-rocket/

24 Longmate, op. cit.

25 Albert Speer, *Inside the Third Reich*, Macmillan, 1970

26 http://www.worldwar2facts.org/v2-rocket-facts.html/

27 Yves Béon, *Planet Dora*, Westview Press, 1997

28 Ibid; Jean Michel, Dora, Holt, Rinehart and Winston, 1979

CONCLUSION

The Nazi regime in Germany lasted a brief 12 years yet in that time it decisively influenced world history – politically, economically and militarily. Its irrational and hateful philosophy did not prevent it from being one of the most advanced scientific nations in the world.

By the end of the war Germany led the world in numerous fields. In aviation, German pilots and planes were the first to break the sound barrier, well before the American Chuck Yeager, who was officially recognized as achieving that feat. Germany developed the most advanced jet aircraft in the world, suction wing aircraft, circular wing aircraft and built and flew the world's first 'stealth aircraft'. In every area of aerospace technology German scientists made radical advances.

In rocketry, German scientists developed the world's first cruise missile and the world's first intercontinental ballistic missile and were the first to enter space. They excelled in the fields of aerospace and astrophysics and laid the foundations of many subsequent developments. The 'space plane' – the

Silbervogel – was the basis of much post-war astrophysical research and played a key role in the development of space exploration. It is no accident that German rocket scientists were eagerly recruited by both the Americans and the Soviet Union to accelerate and develop their space programmes.

In electronics Germans were the first to develop transistors and the first to develop 'over the horizon' radar. They pioneered research into alternative sources of energy and, contrary to popular belief, made huge advances in the field of nuclear physics. Germans were the first to test a 'fizzle' nuclear bomb and may have conducted as many as four successful nuclear tests before the Americans tested their atomic bomb at Los Alamos.

Weaponry was another area in which the Germans led the world. The V-3 – the giant 'super cannon' – was the largest artillery weapon ever devised and if Barnes Wallis's 'bunker bomb' had not destroyed it under ground, it might have rained

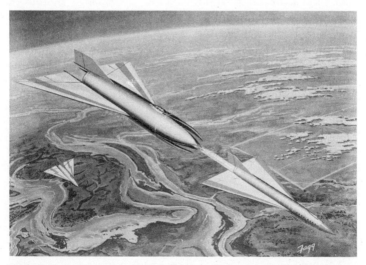

As early as 1929, Austrian scientist Hermann Oberth conceived the idea of a multi-stage rocket as seen in this illustration. Nazi scientists laid the foundations for many later developments in rocketry and aeronautics.

devastation on London. German tanks were some of the best in the world but as well as the ones that saw active service on the front line scientists were developing a variety of exceptionally large and heavy tanks. The most advanced of these projects were the *P-1000 Ratte* and the *P.1500 Monster* tanks. The first weighed 1,000 tons (907 tonnes) and the second 1,500 tons (1,360 tonnes). These two vehicles would have been more like land-based battleships than conventional tanks and would have had a massive firepower with a crew of dozens. The massive weight and the logistics of transporting such large tanks to battle zones made them impractical and although mock-ups of them were designed none of these grandiose visions was ever built. They would certainly have been virtually invulnerable to enemy fire, with only an intense and sustained campaign of heavy bombing able to neutralize them.

In addition to these known 'super tanks' the Germans pioneered a small one-man tank with a spherical shape known as the *Kugelpanzer*. There is little hard data on this project, but the tank finished its journey in Manchuria and was captured by the Soviets. It remains in a Moscow museum and has never been examined by any scientists outside Russia. There is no record of it having been involved in conflict and it remains a fascinating enigma. Was it a pioneering machine that was designed and built and used in action or did it never progress beyond the mock-up stage?

The quality of the conventional German tanks is legendary, although the soldiers of the Wehrmacht were equally surprised at how good the opposing Soviet tanks were. Both nations were certainly responsible for the most advanced tanks in the world during the 1930s and 1940s.

More contentiously, it is possible that German scientists and engineers may have developed the world's first 'flying saucers'. We have seen clear evidence that flying discs were experimented with under the Third Reich. Some variants were essentially versions of helicopters and others were aeroplanes with circular wings but there appear to have been genuinely saucer-shaped vehicles. There is some evidence that a few of these experimental craft made successful test flights and there is considerably more evidence that most of them never flew.

A more dubious claim is that Nazi scientists invented the microwave. It is claimed that during their invasion of the Soviet Union the German troops were equipped with a precursor of the microwave oven known as the radiomissor, which heated up their food in the field. This is generally ridiculed, but the first documented study on the capability of microwaves to cook food was as early as 1946, so the timing makes it just possible. A more serious objection is the poor state of the electrical grid in the Soviet Union during the 1940s, which would have made it difficult for German troops to have obtained sufficient power to operate the machines. It is not impossible, but it is probably unlikely that Nazi soldiers cooked their food in microwaves.[1]

No other regime in history has such a huge and continuing impact on world history after such a brief time in power. The Third Reich's scientific progress, even with the self-imposed handicap of the exile of hundreds of leading German Jewish scientists, was unparalleled and during the war its military capacity was so great that it nearly enabled it to overcome the fundamental problem of being consistently outnumbered by its enemies.

This period in human history is unique and will probably be a source of continuing fascination to historians and the public for centuries to come.

FOOTNOTES

1 Liam S. Whittaker, '15 Mind Blowing Technologies Invented by the Nazis', *CS Globe*, 17 April 2015

INDEX